PET LIBRARY'S

Beagle

Guide

PET LIBRARY'S

Beagle Guide

by John F. Gordon

England

The Pet Library Ltd., Subsidiary of Sternco Industries Inc., 50 Cooper Square, New York, N.Y. Exclusive Canadian Distributor: Hartz Mountain Pet Supplies Limited, 1125 Talbot Street, St. Thomas, Ontario, Canada. Exclusive United Kingdom Distributor: The Pet Library (London) Ltd., 30 Borough High Street, London S.E. 1.

Printed in the Netherlands

Table of Contents

Cover picture: Ake Wintzell

LOUISE VAN DER MEID

Indoors or outdoors, few breeds possess the many attractions offered to the dog lover by the Beagle.

I His Advantages as a Pet

Few breeds possess the many attractions offered to the dog lover by the Beagle. A lively and spirited animal, his "honest" outlook and intelligent approach to man endear him to all with whom he comes into contact. He shows in his eyes and manner a merry disposition which may account for the fact that, like Diogenes, he can adapt himself to life in a barrel or, more fortunately perhaps, to the accepted picture of a perfect baronial home. His distinctive tail flag-waves a buoyant and vital greeting to one and all, yet the Beagle's character and discernment make him choosy of friends beyond the precincts of his own home.

Few dogs are so clean indoors or so easily trained in good manners. His short coat, almost always impeccable, does not litter the house at shedding time, an irritating fault with many of the long-coated breeds. The tidily made feet do not bespatter mud in the home when weather is inclement, nor does the Beagle's small but sturdy frame unduly tax his master's pocketbook when it comes to feeding and general care.

With children he is amiable indeed, often doting upon them, and permitting their unintentionally imposed indignities without resentment. His gay and eager desire for company makes him ever willing to join in their fun, especially when out of doors where he can offer them and his master exhilarating sessions of harmless sport along the country lanes.

And in the hunting pack itself, where his use assumes a more professional aspect, the Beagle's keen nose and tirelessness in the chase render him an efficient game finder and covert-beater. The Beagle is a smart dog in both fashionable and sporting schools; his dutiful manner and polite assurance make him a pleasure to own or work.

The proof of his popularity and ready acceptance into the home life which he increasingly enjoys is witnessed by the vast interest shown in him on both sides of the Atlantic. For many years high in the popularity stakes in the USA, he has pleased his owners and added to domestic bliss in countless family circles. In Britain and many lands overseas, rising figures of registration indicate the confidence felt in him by dog lovers everywhere; for this is a versatile breed with personality, high canine intelligence, and real working ability. As with all functional breeds such as the Beagle, the early existence of pack life, before exhibition work and before pet Beagles were in vogue, stood him in good stead because of the manner of his breeding. Utility (*i.e.*, working) breeds are bred in hard fashion. There is no place in the pack for the physical or temperamental weakling. He is cast out at once and only the strong and able ones are left to procreate their kind.

The hunt must be conducted with "perfect" Beagles, and perfection in the matters of health and efficiency have always been maintained. The strict, often drastic, rule of casting out the dross had its effect in purifying the breed's bloodlines. This resulted in only the best features of this remarkable dog being perpetuated. Present-day owners are benefiting from this perhaps harsh method of selection conducted by the old beaglers, and find with pleasure that, as a result, they have in their Beagles, dogs which possess all the intrinsically sound and likeable attributes that they desire.

What, me lonely?

HOUNDS & HUNTING – H. ARMSTRONG ROBERTS

WIDE WORLD PHOTOS

The Beagle is found everywhere from the humblest cabin to the homes of the mighty. Here President Johnson poses with some new additions to the White House canine corps. Edgar, left, was a gift from FBI Director J. Edgar Hoover. The mother, Freckles, keeps watch over her puppies.

II Origin and History

Research into the obscure beginnings of the Beagle and the origin of its name entails an arduous and perhaps not altogether rewarding task for the historian. Early records show that the Beagle's ancestry stems back to ancient times; some writers suggest that he, or a dog very much like him, hunted with followers of the chase as long ago as 400 BC. They claim that his kind originated in ancient Greece and, bearing in mind that many now-British breeds saw their beginnings in the Mediterranean lands, there can be no reason to discount this theory completely. It is clear, however, that the Beagle's development as we know it was in Great Britain, to which he can certainly claim to be indigenous. Oppianus, poet and historian, who lived some two hundred years after the birth of Christ, wrote

"... there is a certain strong breed of hunting dogs, small, but worthy of sublime song, which the wild tribes of painted Britons maintain." One translator has attempted to introduce the name Beagle into this passage, thus rendering the statement hardly acceptable as an indication of Beagle antiquity, for the name appears to have been evolved many centuries later. Nevertheless, as Oppianus' description stands, it indicates that quite possibly Beagle-type hounds lived and hunted in Britain's primitive days.

How the name "Beagle" was acquired is a subject clouded with conjecture, although a number of feasible explanations have been proffered. Certainly, some attention should be paid to the old Forest Laws of King Canute. These decreed the drastic treatment to be given to dogs trespassing in the royal game forests; fast and powerful breeds such as the Greyhound and Mastiff types were given short shrift. Often cruel treatment such as mutilation of the limbs to deter their activities was proclaimed. It appears, however, that exception was made in the case of a small English dog referred to as the Velterer, known to the English as Langehren (long-eared one). This dog was allowed access to the forest lands, owing to the fact, most probably, that this smallness constituted no menace to the big game which abounded in those days. Another breed, the Ramshundt (Sheepdog), was also exempt from the stringent edict, perhaps because herding would be needed on the forest pastures. It is possible that the Beagle could have been a Langehren, not to be treated rigorously by those who strove to preserve the game.

An interesting study of dog life and some revealing facets of Beagle development can be found in the very scarce *A Treatise and Discourse of the Laws of the Forest*, by John Manwood, published in 1598, which, over its four editions, covers the period between Canute and Queen Anne.

The famous work of Count Gaston de Foix (1331-1391), *Miroir de Phebus*, is of vital interest, for de Foix participated in the great hunts which were popular in his time; his knowledge of the chase in the fourteenth century was unrivalled. The illustration, "Hunting the Fox with Raches," shows hounds (known then as Raches or Rachys) with horsemen and foothunters in full cry. These were apparently Foxhounds, although some writers tell us that the Rach (plural: Rachys) and the Brach (plural: Brachys) terms commonly applied to bitch-hounds, was the Beagle. However, such names were given freely to all dogs who hunted by scent as opposed to those who hunted by sight, and so even the Bloodhound might have been referred to as a Rach in those days. In the legend, *Sir Gawene and the Green Knight* (c.1340), as in other Arthurian stories, one can find reference to the Rach and Brach, but not until 1475 was the Beagle referred to by his own name in *The Squire of Lowe Degre.* We believe this to be the first authentic mention:

> With theyr beagles in that place
> And seven score raches at his rechase.

This points at once, it seems, to the line of demarcation between the Beagle and the Rach, the Rach being the "runner" or "rusher", namely, the larger and faster Foxhound.

Another name which is frequently encountered as the old name for the Beagle is Kenet or Kennet (plural: Kennetys). The word is believed to be from the Old French "kennet", describing a small foot-hound which hunted by scent, referred to in *The Master of Game,* the first work on hunting in the English language. It was written by Edward, second Duke of York, soon after the turn of the fifteenth century, but not published until 1904. It is virtually a translation of de Foix's *Miroir de Phebus,* previously referred to.

The Old French language is also credited with the name Beagle from its "beguelle" (or "begle" in more modern form). Nevertheless, it is frequently difficult to decide whether the English took words from the French, or vice versa. Since "begle" meant small, this small hound may well have been dimly viewed by the great huntsmen of England in those days when large and powerful game, game this hound could never have coped with, was being chased. Possibly some autocratic derision of its diminutiveness was intended in the name Beagle, for the inference of the Old English word was "small – of little value." Of all the explanations for the name of Beagle, this would seem the most reasonable, although a bit irritating perhaps when we consider the high value placed on this grand little dog today.

The fascinating *Boke of St. Albans,* printed about 1486, does not contribute much to Beagle lore, but its author Dame Juliana Berners, the prioress of Sopwell nunnery in Hertfordshire, did list with some authority, we believe, the various breeds then in existence. The prioress' Old English wording is perhaps better given in the modified form of Shakespeare in his *King Lear* (1605):

Mastiff, greyhound, mongrel grim,
Hound or spaniel, brach or lym,
Or bobtail tike or trundle-tail.

Reference to "rachys" and "kennetys" will be found in the *Boke of St. Albans* confirming their existence five hundred years ago.

The name Kennet which we accept without question as the old name for the Beagle is found in ancient records; it was often applied to dogs in the royal kennels. Although the Rach and the Kennet hunted together, being swift and slow hounds respectively in the chase, it is likely that in those far-off days, a deal of inbreeding took place between the two. This would have gone on for many centuries, even from the days when William the Conqueror is supposed to have introduced the Talbot Hound (forebear of the Foxhound and possibly influential in the development of the Beagle) to England. The Talbot was later to be the Old Southern Hound, then the Foxhound, with smaller offshoots eventually to descend as Beagles. Such interbreeding between the sizes would have produced two paths of

On the trail! Notice the determined concentration of these purebred Beagles on the task at hand.

PURINA PET CARE CENTER

preference – one for the larger faster breed, to become the Foxhound, the other fancying a smaller type, eminently suited to small game such as the rabbit, to become the Beagle. We have seen this development with other breeds, the Bulldog and the Schnauzer being two instances from later years, and the Poodle being split into three distinct forms even more recently. It is probable that a trend towards very small Beagles developed and the breed may have gone through a period when it existed merely as a lady's pet, even lap-dog, but upon this phase of history we have no wish to dwell.

In *De Canibus Britannicis* (1570), written by Dr. Johannes Caius, scholar extraordinary and physician-in-chief to Queen Elizabeth I, a serious division of the breeds of dog was attempted for the first time, some sixteen kinds being mentioned, including the Harrier (Hare-chaser), which would have encompassed the Beagle of those days. In Abraham Fleming's *Of Englishe Dogges,* translated from the Latin to English, we find that many breeds received names which described their function as dogs on land or in water. These were Elizabethan days at their best and we are informed that the Queen held the Beagle in high favor, her "glove" or "singing" Beagles presumably being sixteenth century counterparts of those later termed Pocket Beagles. Let us hope, however, that the diminutiveness of the breed was not so extreme as to allow one to be nursed in even the capacious glove or gauntlet of the Elizabethan, as has been suggested by early authors. It is certain that in Elizabeth's period the Beagle was not treated with the seriousness he deserved, and one fears that he was viewed more as a lap-dog than as a sporting hound which was his due. It is said that very small Beagles in France are today termed "Les Beagles Elisabeth", although the name is falling out of use.

The Queen often gave dogs to visiting friends and nobility from abroad. Because of this, many Beagles found homes overseas, and France and Belgium came to know the breed. This may account for the interesting drawing by Johannes Stradanus of Bruges which was published in *Venationes* (1578), engraved by the Galles. It shows a number of small Beagle-type hounds dispatching rabbits against a background of castles and attendant hunters. The Beagle is here described as the "swift English small dog" and the picture gives testimony to the antiquity of the breed. As can be expected, in those days many breeds evinced distinct signs of outcrossing and more infiltration of other strains than we would employ today. Consequently, some of the art renderings resemble Dachshund shadings on the Beagle, rather than pure type, and one is inclined to think some art work was fashioned from hearsay rather than by painters who had actually seen a Beagle! Castiglione, the Genoese (1616-70), depicts a very Beagle-like dog in his "Orpheus", and although it is possible that he could have seen a Beagle on one of his visits to England, it is more probable that he saw a specimen of the breed domiciled in Italy, for by his time the dogs had spread to that land.

The popularity of the Beagle developed greatly with the coming of William II (of Orange) to the throne of England (1689-1702). The king's great hunt at Welbeck was of legendary proportions. It was usual then to employ the Beagle with horse, but the later method of his use as foot hound would appear more likely since he was a comparatively slower working breed. Later Kings of England patronized the Beagle well, King George IV being a great enthusiast. While he was Prince of Wales he maintained a fine pack of Dwarf or Pocket Beagles, although record has it that his strain was adversely criticised as being too mixed and too large, therefore possibly too fast in the chase. This comment came from a well-known figure of the hunting world in those days, one Colonel Thornton, a keen Beagler with a noted pack of Pocket Beagles which he hunted in the southern parts of England. These small dogs were capable of tiring the strongest hunters and returning quite fresh to their kennels, or so we are told in *Sporting Anecdotes* (1807).

Later, Albert, Consort to Queen Victoria, kept a prize pack of tiny pure white Beagles which were regularly put to rabbit. Sporting with these game little dogs assumed in his time almost fashionable proportions amonst the nobility and wealthy farmers. However, towards the close of Victoria's reign, the Beagle's popularity waned, owing largely to the greater use which was made of the Foxhound. The slower hunters of yesteryear were then being replaced with fine thoroughbred horses with greater speed and stamina inbred for the chase. The Beagle, although designed primarily as a foothound, had managed to adapt himself to many hunts where horses were used, but with these faster hunters giving a more rigorous chase, his effectiveness was at last greatly lessened and his popularity suffered.

However, enough stalwarts remained in Beagle circles to ensure that his contribution to the chase and his admirable character were remembered and his breed maintained. Smallness was the criterion of many old Beagle fanciers. Of course, the dogs, although small in

PURINA PET CARE CENTER

The cottontail rabbit frequently takes refuge in dense, tangled blowdown or briars, but the dauntless little Beagle will not be deterred.

frame, had to be packed solid with what is known today as "guts" – meaning that they had to have a full quota of spirit, courage, determination, tenacity and kindred qualities. In the last quarter of the nineteenth century, a number of useful packs hunted the pastoral lands of the southern counties of England, Sussex being quite famous for them. In Dorset, there was an excellent pack owned by a Mr. Crane, and it is said that not one of the dogs exceeded nine inches in height, all being fine specimens. They are described by J. H. Walsh ("Stonehenge") in his *Dogs of the British Isles* (1872).

Those were the days when the scourge of distemper was rife and many good hounds were lost. It virtually wiped out Mr. Crane's pack, which was tragic indeed, for its members would have proved invaluable in the procreation of the breed. Other enthusiasts such as Mrs. C. Chapman of Cheltenham, Mrs. Price of Lyndhurst, and Mrs. J. Cheshire of Watford, as well as Lord Gifford, helped to champion the breed in the south and to preserve its sporting instincts, correct type and size. Beagles which were blue-mottled in coat were seen at one time in Sussex and were often alluded to as Sussex Beagles; some wire or rough coated varieties emanated from the same county.

Rawdon B. Lee in a late edition of his *Modern Dogs* (1906), tells us of the black-and-tan Beagles hunted by the Countess of Lonsdale over the lands of Westmorland about 1902; later they were brought south and sported in Cirencester with a Mr. Kingscote. These lacked the popularity of the more conventional coat owing to the fact that they were less discernible in the field, also because many black-and-tan Beagles were too large.

As with other breeds on which the author has written, the Beagle's pioneers developed its character. Let us say now that there were many more pioneers than can be properly credited in this book, but were it not for the Cranes, the Croftons, the McNutts, and others already mentioned, to name only a few men (and women) who managed their packs with sense, discrimination and instinctive selective ability, the Beagle would not be what he is to-day. These people always kept their eye on the future of the breed. Their wisdom has given us the sound and equable little Beagle we are proud to be owned by today.

The Beagle Club of England

Formed in 1890, this is one of the earliest specialist breed clubs under the wing of the Kennel Club. The name and address of its current secretary will be found at the end of this section and many famous people have held this executive position. The *Beagle Club's Year Book* of 1899 sets out the objects and tenets of the Club.

> *It keeps wide open its doors and welcomes alike to the fold the Master of Beagles who wishes to maintain or form his Pack on ancient lines; the shooting man who keeps a few couples for driving out the rabbits, or putting up the pheasants; the drag hunter who gets an afternoon's healthy exercise with the pleasure of seeing hounds work and hearing hounds music; the exhibitor who finds pleasure in breeding for perfection, so far as looks go and performs most useful work by making the beauty of the breed more generally known; the lady who finds the Beagle the most intelligent and interesting of pets; last, but certainly not least, the old sportsman whose sporting days are over, but who has a keen remembrance of what has been and joins in whilst his recollections and experiences are of inestimable value to a younger generation. All these are now united in the same effort.*

The two World Wars dealt heavy blows to the progress of the Club, as indeed they did to many breed clubs, some falling by the wayside in those years. However, the Beagle Club was fortunate in having Viscount Chelmsford as its backbone during the last war and he navigated it through to the body it is today with a healthy and ever-increasing membership. The Beagle Clubs runs its own specialist breed snow which is well supported.

For further information about the Beagle Club, write to its secretary, Mr. D. J. Webster, Wiltshire House, West Road, Bransgore, Christchurch, Hampshire, England.

The breed's interests are also watched over and maintained by two governing bodies, one being the Kennel Club, the other the A.M.H.B. or Association of Masters of Harriers and Beagles.

The Kennel Club

The English Kennel Club was founded in 1873 in Westminster, London. Its aim was to safeguard the interests of dogs and dog-

Probably tens of thousands of Beagles are kept in America primarily as house dogs, but they are also used for hunting during the season. The vigor and enthusiasm displayed in the field is in sharp contrast to the gentle good nature of the Beagle at home.

PURINA PET CARE CENTER

breeders, its object to promote the improvement of dogs, dog shows and field trials, and in these matters it has been eminently successful. The many malpractices which existed at the time of its formation have been eradicated and the standard of British dogdom is at a very high level. The Kennel Club classifies the many different breeds, maintains a vast registry of pedigreed dogs as well as Associations, Clubs and Societies, formed for the promotion of specialized breeds or varieties of breeds. It licenses dog shows and has formulated careful rules and regulations for the conduct of the dog world which it strictly enforces. It controls the allocation and awarding of Challenge Certificates and Champion Certificates and publishes annually *The Kennel Club Stud Book* and monthly *The Kennel Gazette.*

Beagle pedigrees are recorded in its archives as are the countless registrations in the breed, and the activities of the Kennel Club includes approval of judges at shows where Beagles are exhibited. Only Beagles that are registered at the Kennel Club, or members of a recognized Pack, can be exhibited. To become a Champion, a hound must win three Challenge Certificates, each under a different judge at three distinct championship shows. He can then have the title Champion (or its abbreviation Ch.) entered before his registered name.

The Association of Masters of Harriers and Beagles

The Beagle owes a tremendous debt to the *Beagle Club* also to the Association of Masters of Harriers and Beagles which was formed in 1891, following the success of the Peterborough Hound Show. It became clear at this show that with the Beagle becoming increasingly popular some control of the breed and its packs was essential. All breeds need a controlling influence, otherwise type and uniformity speedily deteriorate. The Association published its first Stud Book some months after inauguration, listing twelve packs. Anyone fortunate enough to possess this first Stud Book and subsequent issues has at his hand an authentic history of the packs from the end of the 19th century, together with fascinating pedigree data, invaluable to the genealogist.

The A.M.H.B. acts as the governing body of Hare Hunting in the British Isles. It runs the Stud Book, in which only Hounds from recognized packs can be entered. The method of entry is simple and revealing. For example, a Hound named "Regent" from the

"Wolverston" pack entered in 1924 would be listed as 'WOLVERSTON REGENT '24".

The Association runs the annual Petersborough Harrier and Beagle Show, and a Hare Hunting Conference which is held every other year. Some thirty Harrier packs and ninety Beagle packs exist – these covering the greater part of England and a large part of Wales, but there are only two packs located in Scotland. The Association keeps a master map on which all packs have their Territory registered so that everyone knows the limits of their boundaries. Masters and officials of all properly constituted packs are welcome as members. It lays down rules for all these activities, and, most important of all, insists that hunting be carried out in a proper manner. The present secretary is Mr. J. J. Kirkpatrick of Rissington Manor, Cheltenham.

It is unfortunate that not all the packs which were active in the period around 1891, when the A. M. H. B. was formed, felt inclined to enter their names in the first Stud Book, so some records are lost. Gerald Massey, famous for his dog books, lists two volumes of the Stud Books, edited by C. W. M. Kemp, compiled by Messrs. Gibbons, Rickards and Humphreys. Volume I covers the year 1891-1900 listing 107 Packs of Harriers and 40 Packs of Beagles. Volume 2, 1901-1910, 91 Packs of Harriers and 69 Packs of Beagles, a fair indication of the sport's development from the entries of twelve packs in the first publication.

The noted Royal Rock pack of Beagles is one of the country's oldest, and although the war stopped its activities to some extent, it can claim an annual event of some kind since its inception in 1845; this is an exceptional record. Its first Master was Mr. C. Rawson and the well-known sportsman, Mr. W. Macfie, also held later office. It is said that the nucleus of the pack was formed from hounds secured from Reverend Honeywood (already referred to), H. Phelps of Buggins Park and Tom Pitt. John Mills in *The Sportsman's Library* (1845), says the Honeywood Pack was the best in Britain at the time. He refers to it as an all white pack, but in the engraving it would seem that the hounds are mainly white or tan or lemon.

The urge to standardize the breed was maintained and individual bloodlines were meanwhile being conserved and developed. Naturally, the different packs favored their own particular type of Beagle – in fact, Mr. W. Macfie, earlier referred to, is purported to have remarked, "I found great difficulty in getting Beagles of hound type. Each Master had a different idea of what a Beagle should be; some had hounds with heads and ears like Fox Terriers, others like pups and some like miniature Foxhounds. . ."

The need for prepotent sires – dogs able to reproduce their own excellent kind – quickly became apparent. With the A. M. H. B. watchful of the Beagle's interest, the dominant stud dogs were quickly noted and the breed began to make good headway with certain sires establishing themselves as notable. One great dog was "Halstead Place Searcher '05" who won the 1905 Champion Cup and produced "Halstead Place Chancellor '07". This dog sired three Champion Cup winners in his turn and the blood of this influential duo ran strongly in most of the best Beagles on the move before World War I. It has filtered through to many of the present-day good ones too.

Pocket Beagle

Whereas the American Kennel Club maintains two classes in its registry, namely, "under 13 inches" and "under 15 inches", the Kennel Club in England has only one size class for the breed, this being "under 16 inches." Until the recent revision of the breed Standard, the "under 10 inches" category was provided for, but since the disappearance of Pocket Beagles in England in the middle thirties there appears no reason for including the tinies.

It is a pity, however, that Pocket Beagles faded away. Many fanciers and huntsmen like them and a desire exists in several regions to revive the variety. It is hoped that its champions will be successful in their endeavors, for this small sporting dog is of great beauty when portrayed well in type. It is not an easy dog to breed true, for varieties controlled by an arbitrary height clause in the Standard frequently produce members which are light in bone, poor in hindquarter development, untypical in head and outlook, and shelly in body properties. Its is not an easy process for the breeder to pack substance and stamina into such a small frame. A Hound has to have endurance and determination in full measure and the Pocket Beagle must conform to the true hound requirements, physically and temperamentally. Smallness in the variety is clearly the desideratum and often the smallest would demand the highest prices. In such a market care had to be taken (and will have to be taken if Pocket Beagles are reinstated) to ensure that the small ones are not mere runts from the standard variety of Beagles. It is, in fact, probably easier to breed small Beagles of proper type and proportions up to 12 inches, than it is to get good 10 inch ones, but when one is bound by firm requirements for height, the skill breeding becomes apparent.

We hope one day to see Pocket Beagles reestablished in Britain. Mrs. Lloyd-Rayner of Ormskirk, who hunted the Fell fox with Dandie Dinmonts and a very fine pack of Pocket Beagles in the beautiful valley of Kentmere (from which name came her prefix), is referred to in the author's monograph on Dandie Dinmont Terriers. She hoped for the perpetuation of her strain, but the rigors of the wars and the effect of the Foxhound mitigated against these hopes and although sometimes one comes across a Hound which savors of the "Kentmere" pack, the true Pocket Beagle seems to be lost to us at this time.

Kerry Beagle

This is a larger Beagle form, often coming to a height of 22 inches. Rather rangier, perhaps, than we have come to prefer in the breed. The Bloodhound influence is apparent, especially in the matter of color – this variety being black and tan.

Used in Ireland for hunting hare, also larger game on occasion, the Kerry Beagle is seldom, if ever, seen in England and not often encounted these days even in the Emerald Isle itself. Although more Foxhound-like than Beagle, he holds the latter's name and is noted for his wonderful voice and great stamina and persistence. Due to his color he is not easy to see while he is working, which is a disadvantage. Packs of Kerry Beagles were established at one time in Killarney and Muckross, but the Scarteen pack seems to have made its mark on posterity, this pack having been established from stock which hunted in Ireland from the middle 18th century. The Ryan family appears to have been closely associated with the variety in these early days.

Rough, or Wire-haired Beagles

Although a keen and efficient hunting variety, these Beagles are not seen today in Britain and some doubt may be cast upon their ancestry. The dog's coarse, dense coat becomes a valuable armor when

While the name Beagle is almost synonymous with "rabbit hound," you can see by this picture that Beagles can be trained to hunt and retrieve birds.

HOUNDS & HUNTING

working in covert, and his ability in the field cannot be questioned. Some terrier or otterhound cross can be suspected, judging from old pictures and the writings of early dog men.

Beagles in the U.S

It is believed that General Richara Kowett of Carlinsville, Illinois, was the first serious importer of Beagles into the United States. As a successful practical, farm stock breeder, the Beagles he purchased had to be good ones, and he set a high standard of quality on his importations. Consequently, the Rowett Beagle developed well with the excellent foundation material that started his strain in the late 1870s. It quickly supplanted the mediocre strains which then existed in several eastern States, which had caused the Beagle to be regarded less favorably than he deserved. With the coming of the new blood and improved type, a surge of interest was aroused, and the Beagle became a sought-after breed. Rowett's Beagles contributed to the establishment of the Waldingfield pack which was formed in 1886 and is America's oldest. Two years later in 1888 the National Beagle Club was inaugurated, its activities coming under the authority of the American Kennel Club. A Standard of the Breed had been formulated just prior to this by General Rowett, Dr. L. H. Twaddell and Mr. N. Ellmore. Since 1887 it has suffered few amendments and reads very much like the English Standard, except in the matter of height where two varieties in height are allowed, while any hound exceeding fifteen inches in height is disqualified.

The Field Trial Beagle

In the United States and Canada the Beagle was slowly increasing in popularity but suddenly, within a few years, there was a sharp spurt in registrations. One highly respected American authority attributes this rise to the correspondingly rapid decline in the popularity of the American Cocker Spaniel. That breed had first position in the AKC registrations when a new vogue in style was developed by show enthusiasts. This involved breeding Cockers with long coats which necessitated regular grooming. Left in the natural state, as were the original American Cockers with their setter type coats, many purchasers turned to the easily cared for Beagle – a dog of similar size and proportion.

The field trial enthusiasts who established several hundred clubs throughout the United States, each club bringing together a group of local breeders, have had an important influence in promoting the breed. The field trial influence has made itself felt in the radical change in appearance of the efficient field trial dog as contrasted with the show type.

Field trial men have thoroughly demonstrated that the type arbitrarily chosen as a show type is completely outclassed as a hunting dog by the field trial type which has developed through competition. The latter have shorter necks and a more cobby appearance. In a dog show in England or the United States a dog which has demonstrated his efficiency in the field might make show enthusiasts wonder it was not of a different breed.

Thus a cleavage has divided the two groups. The field trial men believe the show standard should depict a Beagle which is most efficient at the Beagles' business – running rabbits. The show group is interested only in the idea of a beautiful Beagle, regardless of hunting ability.

Bryn Mawr Hound Show

The Peterborough Hound Show, so popular in England, has as its equivalent in America the Bryn Mawr Hound Show. This is held every year, and is well supported. One can have little doubt that Beagles in America have made their mark. Some will say that Beagles in the USA are better than their English cousins. Comparisons are always invidious, but it is true that standards of Beagle quality are high in America and some departments of the breed's make up are generally superior to those of British dogs. On the other hand, Britain's Beagles have much to offer in return.

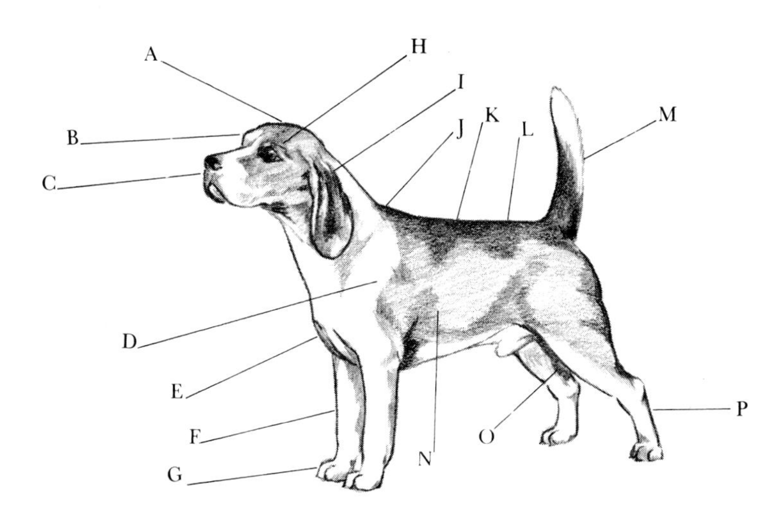

A) Skull - domed and moderately wide
B) Stop - well defined
C) Muzzle - medium lenght and not snipy. Lips well flewed
D) Shoulders - sloping, clean and muscular
E) Chest - deep and moderately broad
F) Forelegs - straight, plenty of round bone. Elbows neither in nor out
G) Feet - close, round and firmly padded
H) Eyes - kindly, mild expression
I) Ears - set on low and close to head. Rounded at tip
J) Withers - fine
K) Back - short, strong, level and muscular
L) Loin - broad and powerful
M) Tail - set high and carried gaily. Not curled over back
N) Ribs - well sprung
O) Stifles - strong and well turned
P) Hocks - well let down, turning neither in nor out

PRUDENCE WALKER

Points to look for in a Beagle.

III Standard of the Breed

Here are the American and English Standards of the Breed for the Beagle, published here through the courtesy of the American Kennel Club and The Kennel Club (England). Further on, there is a more detailed discussion by the author of the various "wanted" points. Not even a skilled breeder can always predict how a puppy is going to develop, but in our chapter on Selecting a Beagle I point out some of the traits, both positive and negative, to look for in the young dog.

The American Standard

General Appearance: *A miniature Foxhound, solid and big for his inches, with the wear-and-tear look of the hound that can last in the chase and follow his quarry to the death.*

Head: *The skull should be fairly long, slightly domed at occiput, with cranium broad and full. Ears – Ears set on moderately low, long, reaching when drawn out nearly, if not quite, to the end of the nose; fine in texture, fairly broad – with almost entire absence of erectile power – setting close to the head, with the forward edge slightly inturning to the cheek – rounded at tip. Eyes – Eyes large, set well apart – soft and houndlike – expression gentle and pleading; of a brown or hazel color. Muzzle – Muzzle of medium length – straight and square-cut – the stop moderately defined. Jaws – Level. Lips free from flews; nostrils large and open. Defects – A very flat skull, narrow across the top; excess of dome, eyes small, sharp and terrierlike, or prominent and protruding; muzzle long, snipy or cut away decidedly below the eyes, or very short. Roman-nosed, or upturned, giving a dish-face expression. Ears short, set on high or with a tendency to rise above the point of origin.*

Body – Neck and Throat: *Neck rising free and light from the shoulders strong in substance yet not loaded, of medium length. The throat clean and free from folds of skin; a slight wrinkle below the angle of the jaw, however, may be allowable. Defects – A thick, short, cloddy neck carried on a line with the top of the shoulders. Throat showing dewlap and folds of skin to a degree termed "throatiness". Shoulders and Chest – Shoulders sloping – clean, muscular, not heavy or loaded – conveying the idea of freedom of action with activity and strength. Chest deep and broad, but not broad enough to interfere with the free play of the shoulders. Defects – Straight, upright shoulders. Chest disproportionately wide or with lack of depth. Back, Loin and Ribs – Back short, muscular and strong. Loin broad and slightly arched, and the ribs well sprung, giving abundance of lung room. Defects – Very long or swayed or roached back. Flat, narrow loin. Flat ribs.*

Forelegs and Feet – Forelegs: *Straight, with plenty of bone in proportion to size of the hound. Pasterns short and straight. Feet – Close, round and firm. Pad full and hard. Defects – Out at elbows. Knees knuckled over forward, or bent backward. Forelegs crooked or Dachshundlike. Feet long, open or spreading.*

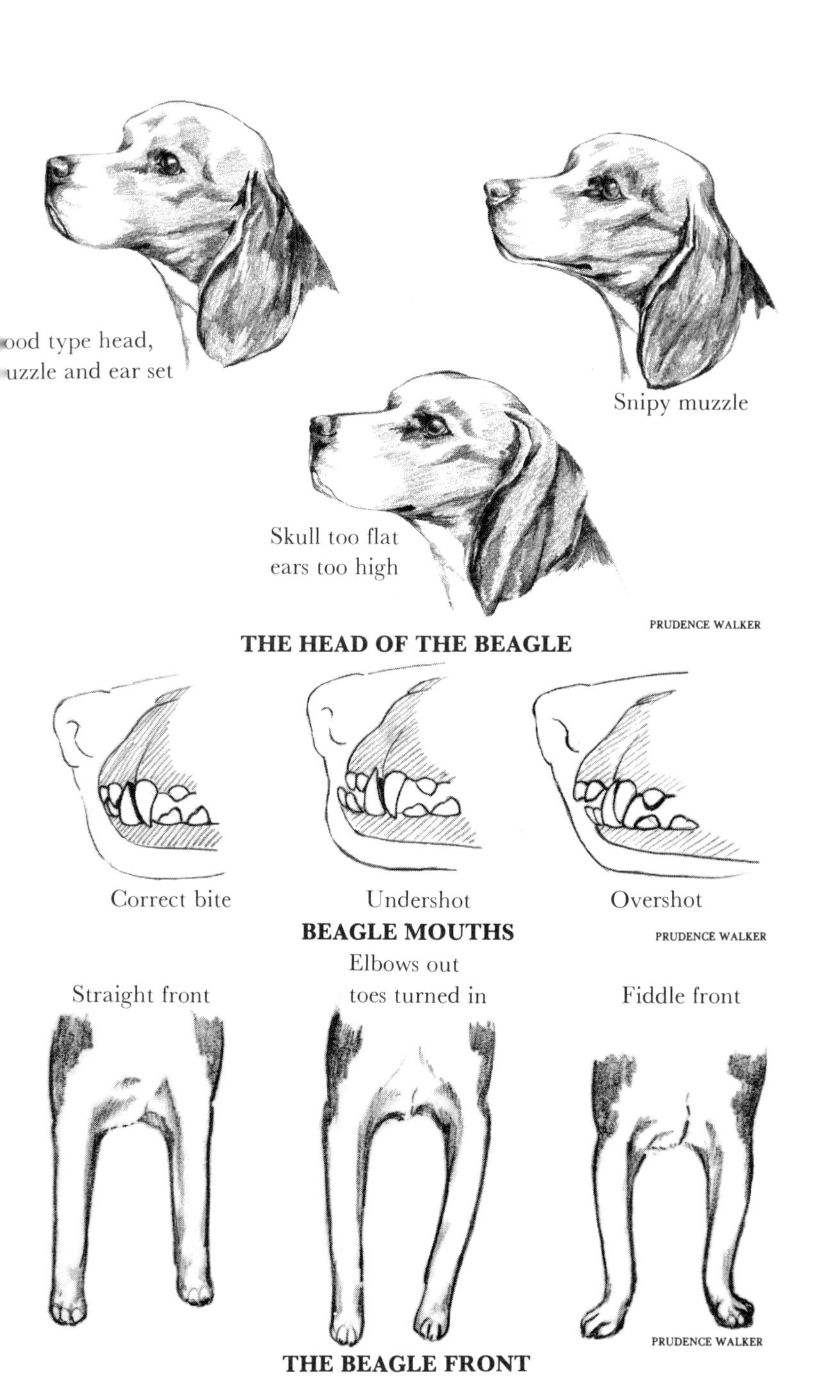

THE HEAD OF THE BEAGLE

BEAGLE MOUTHS

THE BEAGLE FRONT

Hips, Thighs, Hind Legs and Feet: *Hips and thighs strong and well muscled, giving abundance of propelling power. Stifles strong and well let down. Hocks firm, symmetrical and moderately bent. Feet close and firm. Defects – Cowhocks, or straight hocks. Lack of muscle and propelling power. Open feet.*
Tail: *Set moderately high; carried gaily, but not turned forward over the back; with slight curve; short as compared with size of the hound; with brush.*
Defects: *A long tail. Teapot curve or inclined forward from the root. Rat tail with absence of brush.*
Coat: *A close hard, hound coat of medium length. Defects – A short, thin coat, or of a soft quality. Color – Any true hound color.*
Varieties: *There shall be two varieties. Thirteen Inch – which shall be for hounds not exceeding 13 inches in height. Fifteen Inch – which shall be for hounds over 13 but not exceeding 15 inches in height.*

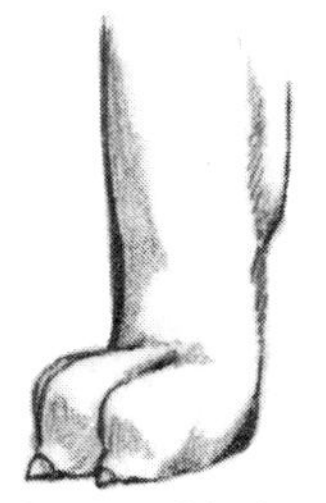

Correct hind end

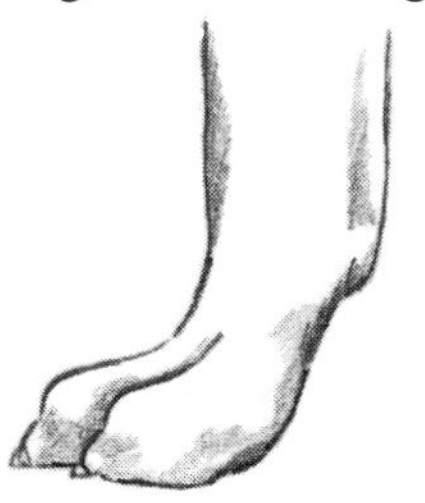

Hare foot

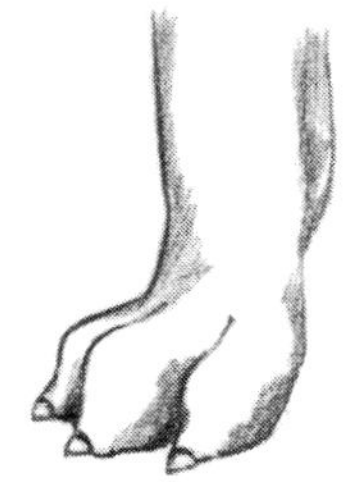

Splay foot

PRUDENCE WALKER

THE BEAGLE FOOT

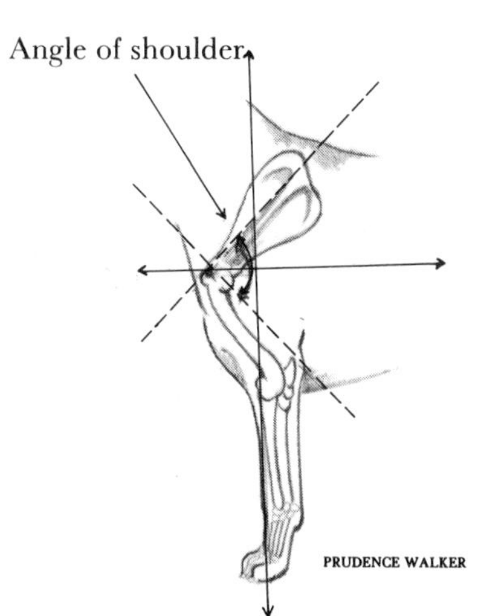

The skeletal structure making for a proper shoulder.

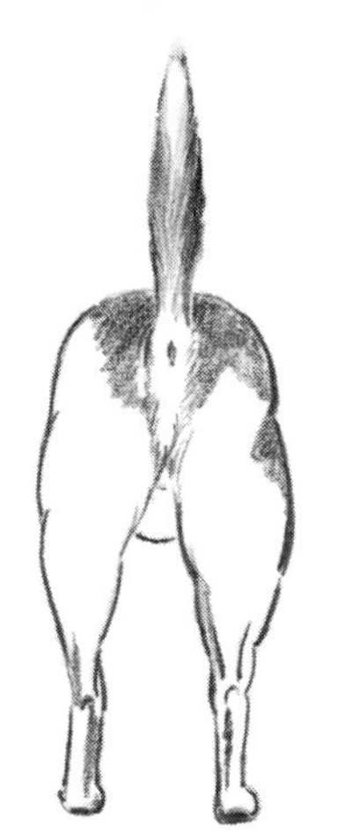

Correct round cat foot

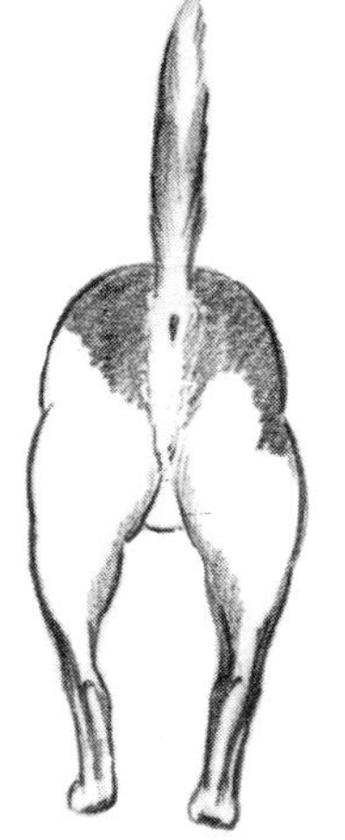

In-toed

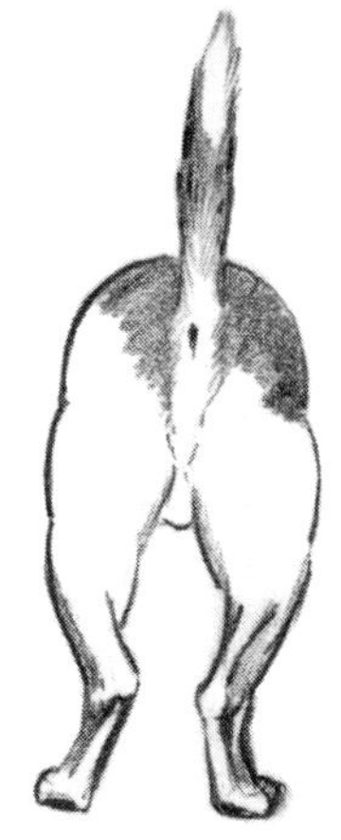

Cow hocked

PRUDENCE WALKER

THE BEAGLE FROM THE REAR

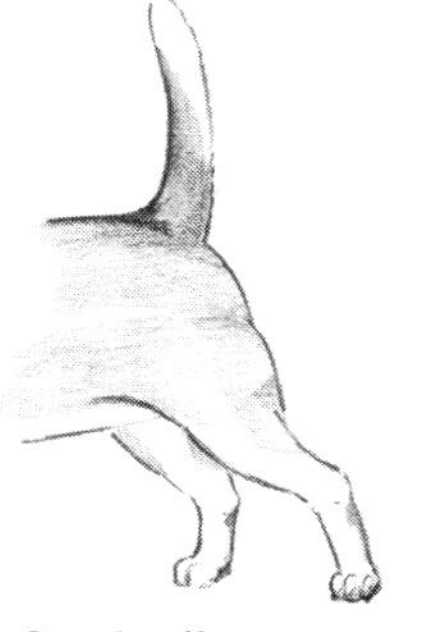

Good tail set and carriage

Tail set and carriage too low

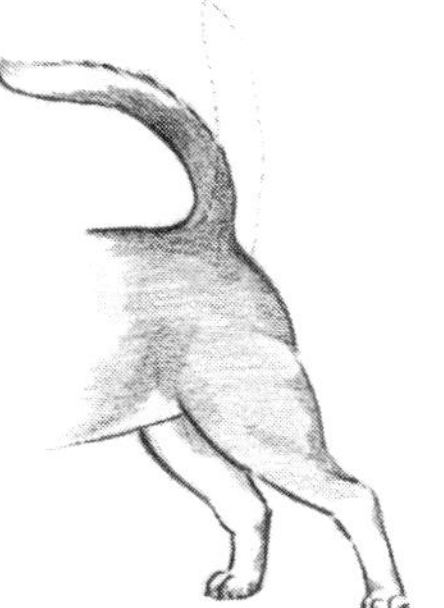

Sickle tail and set too high

PRUDENCE WALKER

CORRECT TAIL CARRIAGE

Scale of Points

Head		
Skull	5	
Ears	10	
Eyes	5	
Muzzle	5	25
Body		
Neck	5	
Chest and shoulders	15	
Back, loin and ribs	15	35
Running Gear		
Forelegs	10	
Hips, thighs and hind legs	10	
Feet	10	30
Coat	5	
Stern	5	10
Total		100

Disqualification

Any hound measuring more than 15 inches shall be disqualified.

The English Standard

General Appearance: *A compactly built Hound without coarseness, conveying the impression of great stamina and activity.*
Head and Skull: *Head fair length, powerful without being coarse, skull domed, moderately wide with an indication of peak; stop well-defined, muzzle not snipy and lips well-flewed. Nose black, broad and nostrils well expanded.*

Typical male head
(Note more width between ears than female, heavier muzzle, deeper before eyes and cheerier)

Typical female head
(Softer expression 'cleaner' look of muzzle, cheek and neck)
PRUDENCE WALKER

The head of the male Beagle (left) differs from that of the female. There is more width between the ears, a heavier muzzle; it is deeper between the eyes and cheekier. The typical female has a soft expression, with a cleaner look on the muzzle, neck and cheek.

Eyes: *Brown, dark hazel or hazel, not deep set or bulgy and with a mild expression.*
Ears: *Long, set on low, fine in texture and hanging in a graceful fold close to the cheek.*
Neck: *Moderately long, slightly arched, and throat showing some dewlap.*
Forequarters: *Shoulders clean and slightly sloping. Forelegs quite straight, well under the dog, of good substance and round in bone.*
Body: *Short between the couplings, well let down in chest, ribs fairly well sprung and well ribbed-up. Loins powerful and not tucked up.*
Hindquarters: *Very muscular about the thighs; stifles and hocks well bent and hocks well let down.*
Feet: *Round, well knuckled up and strongly padded.*

Tail: *Of moderate length, set on high, and carried gaily, but not curled over the back.*
Coat: *Smooth variety: Smooth, very dense and not too fine or short. Rough variety: Very dense and wiry.*
Color: *Any recognised Hound Color.*
Weight and Size: *Height should not exceed 16 inches.*

This dog is slightly overshot, that is, the teeth in the upper jaw project too far beyond those in the lower.

Interpreting the Beagle Standard

This is one of the most concise of the breed Standards. It was formed in the nineteenth century by lovers and experts of the breed and remains today more or less unaltered. It is a good description of a good dog. It has no embellishments, for neither the Beagle nor his admirers require them. It creates a perfect word picture to guide those striving to produce the perfect Beagle. It is a difficult task to get even within striking distance of the *beau ideal.* Sometimes a breeder thinks he has it; often his enthusiasm has been found to have overridden his judgment. Certainly, many great dogs and bitches have been bred in England and America in the last few score years, some near, in their excellence, to the perfect state. That some margin remained for the improvement of the Beagle ideal cannot, unfortunately, be denied. In common with most other breeds, perfection has yet to be produced in the Beagle world.

The Standard of the Beagle is written to describe the perfect specimen. Nevertheless, opinions vary. If they did not, then where would be the fun in dog showing? It would soon die a natural death if every judge saw things the same way, and the same dogs in competition were repeatedly placed in the same winning order. Of course, where really first class specimens are involved, the degree of variation in judging is slight. It is this variation in the interpretation of the Standard and the difference in opinion which occurs with judges that adds the "spice" to exhibition work. Indeed, it is essential in order to maintain enthusiasm among breeders and fanciers generally.

Sound opinion as to what constitutes a good Beagle can only come from a judge who has either owned good Beagles himself or mixed extensively with good ones in Beagle circles. It is necessary for a judge to retain in his mind an image of the best and outstanding features of every great Beagle he meets. By doing this, he builds up in his consciousness a picture of the perfect Beagle. Upon each dog he assesses he will superimpose this paragon's image and from his decisions will be revealed his particular interpretation of the Standard.

Some judges learn the art slowly, others seem to have an instinctive "eye for a dog" and display their ability sooner. No judge can be worthy unless he realizes that each section of the Standard has its own particular value or importance to the make up of the Beagle. He must learn that each and every one of the various points in the Standard have to come together towards a pleasing and satisfactory whole Beagle. It must be realized a specimen can possess a beautiful head, a fine body, a perfect tail and, in fact, be ideal in all departments, but if these parts are not molded well into each other in structural excellence, then that animal can be of no worth.

The Beagle is a functional dog. He functions as a Hound, needing great energy and stamina. He has to possess strength and power, to be indifferent to physical discomfort, and he *must* be constructed properly to do his job. If the dog you judge is not patently able by virtue of his size, construction and outlook to perform his task effectively in the field, then he is not much good. No person should aspire to judge Beagles unless he has been out with the pack, watching the hounds go and seeing what they do in the field. This is where information can be gleaned. Pearls of wisdom can be collected from the talk of knowledgeable huntsmen and old-timers – the student will learn quickly enough when and how to sort the wheat from the chaff. He will learn too that the best judges are impartial. Personal "feelings" have no place in the fair assessment of a specimen. It is overall quality, with no exaggerations, one looks for – complete soundness in structure and movement, and judgment by good points rather than the negative method of counting up the faults!

The Beagle Standard is now reviewed point by point:

The ideal Beagle as painted by Prudence Walker.

General Appearance

The general appearance of the Beagle can help him or damn him in the show ring. Many judges take their first impressions from the exhibits as they enter the ring to be judged. A bad appearance, perhaps formed by indifferent conditions – an untidy entrance or more serious, some weakness in breed type may be discerned immediately. It is wise to start "showing" your dog even as you approach the ring, so that both you and the dog had best be on your toes. A Beagle scoring in good general appearance is one abounding with breed type, pleasing balance and confident stance and gait. The exhibit should be in superb show condition, with a clean, sparkling coat. Bone should be ample and body well put together and harmoniously to make a pleasing picture.

Head and Skull

The head is the hallmark of the Beagle. The length and breadth and depth must bear distinct relation with each other to achieve a perfect balance; then in turn the headpiece must balance with the body of the Hound. The lip should be square in appearance under the nose and not overdone to the point of lippiness. Coarseness in skull lends an unpleasant aspect as does a mean head. The stop should be distinct; any lack of indentation here creates an untypical appearance. A black nose is asked for in the Standard and this is ideal, but dogs with a predominance of white or lemon in their coats can be permitted some leeway in this department as they frequently lack pigmentation in the nose. The mouth should be what is known as the "level" mouth. This gives the conventional scissor bite. It is formed so that the upper incisors rest over and upon the surface of the lower incisors. Lastly, learn to assess the difference between the ideal head of a dog (male) and that of the bitch. The latter should look feminine. For a bitch to look doggy is a fault, but not as bad as an overrefined male, lacking essential masculinity.

Eyes

Beagle expression is a vital matter. It should be mild, although clearly intelligent, and alert. Anything which savors of the varmint is unwanted in the breed. The true Beagle expression can be obtained only if the eyes are bred to the right color, which is brown, dark hazel or hazel. Light eyes, although seen quite frequently, are not desirable. These usually indicate shrewdness as opposed to the fine temperament of their dark eyed brothers. The emplacement of the eyes is quite important too, close set eyes mitigating against general appearance. Eyes which are bulbous or protuberant are objectionable. Not only do they bestow a vapid expression, but they are vulnerable to damage when the dog is passing through rough cover.

One of the fine Beagles being bred in Sweden today. There are many rabbits in the forests and "Beagling" is a popular sport.

AKE WINTZELL

Ears

The ideal length of ear in the Beagle is that which reaches almost to the nose tip. The carriage of the ears should be so that they lie close to the cheek and set on at a point of the skull which is on an even line with the temporal canthus of the eye or slightly below it. The Beagle's ears are not noted for their movement and this, in fact, should be slight even when his attention is attracted. Ear texture plays an important part in the carriage of the ear; coarse or heavy leathers never hanging properly, often falling away from the cheek or by virtue of their weight hanging too low, give an impression of faulty set-on. The Standard demands the ears should hang in a graceful fold. This fold should be at the top of the ear, and where the ear ends this should be rounded cleanly and flat, showing its full width.

Neck

The Beagle should have ample reach of neck. It should be moderately arched at the crest and of a length to allow him to come down comfortably to scent. It should be strongly made to support and administer the head as befits the proud Beagle and with sufficient room to give good cry. An overlong neck lacks strength, and one which is too short carries more dewlap than is required in the Beagle.

Forequarters

The forelegs should be straight and with ample bone right down to the feet, with no looseness at the shoulders. The front legs should be parallel with enough space between to allow good chest development. The elbows should not turn out but should lie nicely against the side walls of the chest. Balance should be good when viewed from the front. (This is just as important as balance in profile.) A hound which is leggy lacks balance; one which is too short in leg must sacrifice some agility and balance at the same time.

Body

The Standard offers a good description of body requirements. The Beagle's must be powerful and muscular in its small frame, yet possess quality. He should have a big rib cage to allow plenty of heart room and to support his respiratory machinery. The brisket should be deep and the chest line coming down at least an inch below the point of elbow. The sides and loins need to be nicely muscled-up with no evidence of fat, which will slow up even the best of Beagles. Topline should be level, the couplings compact. Bad faults are the sway back, which is evidenced by a dip behind the shoulders and the roach back, which is shown as a convex backline, commencing from a dip at the withers to another dip at the set-on of the tail. This is particularly objectionable in the breed, and the fault is usually accompanied by proppy shoulders.

Hindquarters

These should be nicely muscled up, hard to the touch, but not tight and bunchy. This is often a strong form of muscle but it is not ideal. Far better for the hindquarters to be made with long well-toned muscle for they endure longer. Correct bone structure is important, giving well-bent stifles and hocks which are well let down. The development of the second thighs is important too, for a dog's hindquarters control his dynamic activity and well-formed ones allow full elasticity of movement. Again, balance has to be seen in the matter of height and breadth of the hindquarters when viewed from the rear. Cow-hocks (when the point of the hocks turn in towards each other) are weaknesses, as are "in-toes", when the points of hock turn outwards and feet turn in. Whereas, possibly some concession might be allowed to a Beagle with "in-toes" (or "pin-toes" as they are sometimes called) in the forequarters, the point is a faulty one, more serious at the rear end of the dog. Straight stifles indicate weakness in the propelling machinery and may well contribute to some failing in the patella area. Too much muscle development on the posterior is liable to cause degeneration, and any substantial build-up of muscle in this region should be avoided.

Feet

A Hound needs to have good feet to do his work properly in the field. The Beagle's feet should be well knuckled up, round and strongly padded. They should be neat, tidy feet, rather like those of the cat. Thin, flat feet with splayed digits are objectionable and certainly of no use to the Hound.

SALLY ANNE THOMPSON

The soulful look of the Beagle conceals the gay spirit within; this has earned him the title of "the merry little hound".

Tail

The Beagle's tail is a vital facet in his make up. It is a shortish appendage, strongly set on, with a substantial root where it joins the body, and with a good brush. Breeders like to see a white tip and generally prefer the shorter stern to the nevertheless correct longer variety. A low set tail is bad and occurs in dogs that are inclined to fall away at the croup. The screw or pigtail, also the ring tail, are unsightly faults and these are transmittable in breeding.

Coat

The Beagle, being a sporting breed, requires a coat capable of keeping out the weather. Consequently, a dense, smooth and possibly not too short coat is indicated. Fine hair coats and coarse coats are the extremes and neither are particularly effective. Rough-coated Beagles are seldom, if ever, seen today in Britain, but the early specimens had coats which were particularly effective in thwarting the weather and the buffeting of covert work.

Color

Most people prefer the black blanket tricolors (black and white with tan trim), but the popular fancy may extend to other coat colors. The lemon-and-white; tan-and-white and the various pieds, also blue-mottle; liver-tan-and-white are the other coat colors most likely to be seen. The last named color variety is considered objectionable by many fanciers, especially exhibitors. This may be due to the fact that so many are light in eye. Hounds which are all white are very nice, some of the old packs specialized in them. As with other breeds which turn up all white, pigmentation is sometimes suspect, and it is therefore necessary to maintain good dark points, for instance, nose, eye, eye-rims and lips-rims color in this coat variety. The blue-mottle or blue-tick is an attractive coat and one which originated in the early Beagles. In it a blue fleck mark is distributed on a light coat.

Weight and Size

The height of the Beagle should not exceed 16 inches and with this height the Beagle should be visually well-balanced.

As mentioned already, judging should be done positively on the good points of the dog rather than in the negative manner of seeking out the faults first. The latter system is inclined to lower the average level of the breed to sound but typeless individuals. Again, no judge should confine himself to solitary points of excellence, such as good heads, forgetting meanwhile the rest of the dog's body, overlooking his temperament in the process. Some breeds have suffered by just those methods of judging; a few have deteriorated almost to their downfall by over-zealous attention to faddist points.

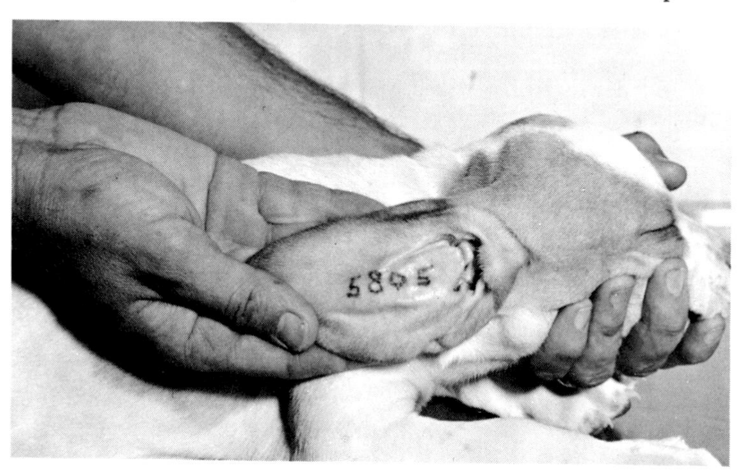

PURINA PET CARE CENTER

Today, many dogs, particularly those which hunt in packs, are painlessly tattooed for permanent indentification.

SALLY ANNE THOMPSON

English Champion Rossut Triumphant, the top British Beagle of all time. with 23 Kennel Club Challenge Certificates, all awarded under different judges. Before purchasing a Beagle, a beginner should consult books on the breed, get to know the required Standards, and study top-winning Beagles such as this one carefully.

IV Selecting a Beagle

If you seek a first class puppy, either you or the friend you take along to help you select a good one should have had a fair sprinkling of personal experience with the breed. Admittedly there have been instances of people with no knowledge of Beagles who have been fortunate enough to pick a champion, but this is a "hit-and-miss" system which seldom proves itself even once in a lifetime.

A beginner should first study books on the breed, get to know the standards, and discuss points, good and bad, with fanciers who know Beagles. It goes without saying that it is necessary to learn from people who *really* know their subject. There are many in dogdom who *think* they know what they are talking about, but fail sadly when their knowledge is put to the test. The novice should attend as many Beagle specialty shows as he can. All-breed shows where Beagles are included are useful, but specialty shows where only Beagles are included are more valuable. Championship shows, in particular, are valuable, for here one can expect to find the cream of Beagles – to see specimens that are champions of their breed and typical of the points currently in vogue. Most Beagle exhibitors will have a ready word of advice for the beginner; most owners of good dogs will allow him to go over their winners, and any opportunity

SALLY ANNE THOMPSON

As well as the black, white and tan called tricolor, Beagles come in blue, tan and white and, as we see here, lemon and white. Beagle puppies are adorable in any color.

to do this should be eagerly accepted for much can be learned from the "feel" of a good dog.

In America there is a wide difference in appearance between the show and the field trial Beagle. In deciding on a dog one should first ask, "What do I want the dog for – pet, show, field trial or just a personal hunting dog?"

Some show dog types make fairly satisfactory hunters, but for outdoor competition one should look up the owners of field trial dogs and buy one of theirs. Attend a large field trial and observe the winners; there is no better way of learning who has the best dogs.

Leading kennels may be visited. Most Beagle fanciers will be pleased to show you their great specimens and discuss their points. Questions will usually be answered helpfully, but the novice should take care that he does not make a nuisance of himself. He should remember when he visits a successful kennel that the development of its winning strain has not come easily. No doubt much hard work, planning, and money has gone into it – many disappointments too as top breeders know only too well. Therefore, any item of information gleaned from such as source is something to be cherished and appreciated. The hard way of learning a subject is to stumble a few times while progressing. If you avoid these pitfalls you are fortunate indeed, and if you can do this by learning from others' mistakes by all means do so. Before too long, you will be able to pass on your experience to other novices, anxious to learn about Beagles.

Pet Shops

Many city dwellers do not have ready access to kennels, and for these people pet shops offer a convenient source for purchasing pet stock. A larger pet shop will almost always have a number of specimens of a popular breed like the Beagle from which the prospective purchaser can make a selection. A reliable pet shop will, in addition, provide a written health guarantee which provides for approval of the dog by a veterinarian (within a reasonable time limit) before the sale becomes final.

A conveniently located pet shop is also advantegeous in that it is a ready source of professional help and instruction during those first few weeks when untutored pup and amateur owner are learning to adjust to each other.

SALLY ANNE THOMPSON

Leading kennels may be visited. Most Beagles fanciers will be pleased to show you their great specimens and discuss their points.

Making Your Choice

When you feel that you are ready to make your choice, and have the money in your pocket, go to a Beagle breeder or a dealer with a reputation for integrity. Ask to see the litter from which you hope to choose your puppy. You will be wise to insist on seeing a complete litter. If you are shown just two or three puppies it is quite possible that the best ones have already been sold, or are being withheld from sale. This is a perfectly legitimate procedure, of course, for every kennel wishes to maintain its strain and keep a few potential show winners. However, it is not good to be limited in your choice and so it might be better to wait until you have at least six puppies to choose from.

The best age at which to make your choice is when the puppies are nine or ten weeks old. First, watch them playing. Some will at once endear themselves to you; others you will pass by because either instinctively you do not consider them attractive or you spot some defect. Let them play about for five minutes at least. Take your time; it is your money and the puppy will be yours for some time to come, let us hope. Try and get a promising puppy to move in a straight line away from you so that his front and forward gait are observable. Badly formed limbs and poorly placed shoulders will not improve with age, and a youngster built indifferently is no bargain. Next, pick up the puppy and place him firmly but gently on a flat surface level with your chest. In this position you can handle him conveniently, and check his good points.

Points to Look For When Choosing a Beagle

1. Massive build in a compact frame.
2. Strong, typical head with a definite stop, strong for face, nicely squared off muzzle, well endowed with lip.
3. Ample, round bone running down to well-knit feet.
4. Good eye emplacement, that is, with enough width between the eyes to render the expression typical.
5. Level mouth, that is, with the upper incisors resting over and upon the lower incisors. However, with very young puppies, a slight space between the two rows of teeth can be allowed for lower jaw development.
6. Stern of correct length, set on in the right place and carried gaily. The finger and thumb should be run down the tail from set-on to tip, sides and top and bottom, to establish no evidence of kink.

The above, of course, applies to anyone wanting a typy show dog. By ten weeks the body conformation will have developed enough to help you choose the puppy which will probably be the best in the litter.

Now, if it is a pet you desire, pick your puppy at an earlier age – 5 or 6 weeks, no later, unless you can be assured that the puppy has been handled a great deal by its owner. It is more trouble but well worth the extra effort, as any psychologist will agree. The younger puppy makes a better pet, seldom becomes shy, providing you handle it properly.

Many people do not have ready access to kennels, and for them pet shops offer a convenient source for purchasing pet stock.

LOUISE VAN DER MEID

The best age at which to make your choice is when the puppy is 9 or 10 weeks old. Some will at once endear themselves to you.

SALLY ANNE THOMPSON

SALLY ANNE THOMPSON

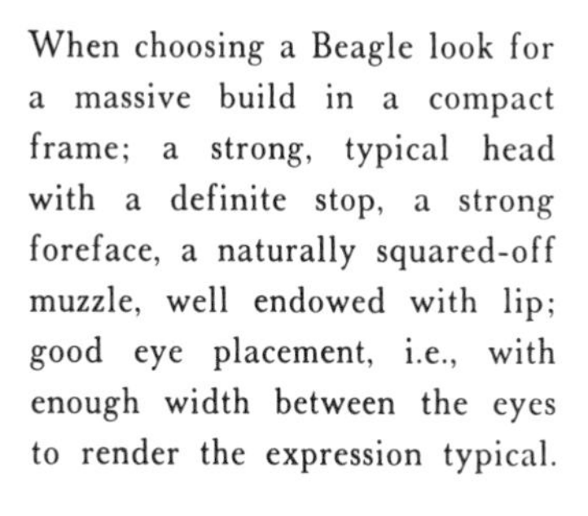

When choosing a Beagle look for a massive build in a compact frame; a strong, typical head with a definite stop, a strong foreface, a naturally squared-off muzzle, well endowed with lip; good eye placement, i.e., with enough width between the eyes to render the expression typical.

TOM CARAVAGLIA

American Champion Johnson's Fancy Boots. Fine stud dogs like this produce the type of puppy which we would all like to own.

Once the visual examination has been completed and you have satisfied yourself on the puppy's strong points, consider his mental traits. This is no easy task but an effort should be made to confirm that your puppy possesses sound and typical Beagle character. First, the youngster should be sprightly and versatile in manner. The fact that he does not rush up to you and exude friendliness should not put you off. Many intelligent puppies are prudent in their choice of friends. This inbred caution is often a good thing and a pup so endowed should receive your approbation, not your distrust. Of course, if a puppy quakes in a corner and is clearly possessed with some inborn nervous tendency, he cannot be of use to you. You will have to use your common sense to decide whether the puppy is nervous or merely cautious. It should not be difficult to determine. To a large extent, an examination of the puppy's parents will guide you. It may not be possible to see the sire, for he may be a stud dog not connected with the breeding kennel, but the dam should be there for you to observe. Check her points and temperament, both of which are apparent in a mature specimen.

What to Avoid

Your considerations so far have been on positive points, that is, the puppy's virtues. This is the correct way to judge livestock – good points first, faults second. However, certain faults cannot be ignored, even in a puppy that has some better than average positive points. A youngster with a doubtful mouth should be left behind if you want a show dog. An undershot specimen is viewed askance by any conscientious judge, and such a dog will never get far in competition. Feet are important in a Beagle, so beware of the forefeet that turn out unduly. Such feet are bad in a small puppy for as the animal matures they well may worsen. It is best to have straight front legs coming down to feet more or less in a straight line. From the time the puppy is up and about after weaning, every attention to good foot development should have been given by the breeder. Trying to correct bad feet later on is a Herculean task.

Nose pigmentation in a Beagle liberally coated in white or lemon often worries the inexperienced buyer, for so many small puppies have "butterfly" noses when the nostrils are mottled or show flesh color. However, as in Beagle eye color, so often suspect in two-monthers, nose color will usually correct itself within a few months. Neither characteristic should occasion worry for they are slight hazards. Check the puppy's bone and tail carriage. Faults, if they exist in these departments, are transmittable in breeding and should make you reconsider your choice.

Physical Check

Reject a puppy who seems underfed or whose eyes and nose are mucousy. A sick puppy will often have a dull glassy-eyed look in contrast to the bright, shiny, gamin look of a healthy dog. Do the ribs feel bony or is there a reassuring layer of flesh between them and the skin? Feel the stomach to make sure that it is not just a bloated belly.

Look at the teeth and gums. Teeth should be clean and white, and not pitted. Gums should be pink. Look into the ears. Are they free of any sign of infection or inflammation? Examine the belly for flea bites, pustules, and the possibility of an umbilical hernia. This will show itself as a small blisterlike protrusion in the middle of the abdomen.

The skin and coat should be examined for any sign of bare patches, rawness, scabs, possible skin disease. Take a pinch of skin and pull it up – gently, of course – and note whether it snaps back into place. A healthy skin is always elastic.

Male or Female?

The decision as to whether to buy a male or female often confuses the potential owner choosing a pet. Much depends on what the dog is wanted for and the conditions that exist for keeping it. Most people, buying a puppy for the first time, choose a male. They feel that males constitute the least trouble. It is true that a bitch with her periodic heat cycles (twice a year) needs extra care and attention, but today this drawback is less than it once was. There are several commercial preparations on the market that help to nullify the bitch's scent during the menstrual period. With this single disadvantage corrected, the female can be considered as equally desirable as her opposite sex.

For those who require an outstanding example of the show Beagle, then clearly the male has to be their choice. He will evince all the positive characteristics of the breed without question. If you have a fine specimen, he is more than likely to make a name for himself at shows. Other Beagle owners will want to breed him to their bitches, and your dog will be contented with his sex life, and thrive.

But if yours is only a run-of-the-mill specimen, or if you live in an isolated environment where females are scarce, or even non-existent, then you may find him a disturbed dog with the coming of puberty. In the family circle, a male so frustrated can prove an embarrassment to his master and to visitors. For this reason alone, many owners prefer the female. With her seasons dealt with effectively, they feel that the female is more loyal, makes a better watchdog, and is generally more pleasing to have around the house. Certainly a number of people, originally owners of males, seek the female for their second dog, and it is said that once a person has owned a female he never again prefers a male.

It would appear then that a female is to be preferred. One must however consider his living environment. It is pointless to take in a female if you live on open property for then she can be approached too readily by stray males who will cause unwanted pregnancies. A male might well wander in such an environment, but at least he would wander exploratively and at his own pace, finding his way home in due course. A straying bitch, on the other hand, harassed and chased into areas beyond her ken, is likely to be lost or stolen.

Expert breeders usually advise the ownership of a female for the one dog owner. Kennel owners themselves frequently choose a female for their house pet.

When selecting a male, pay particular attention to his genitals. Make sure that he has two testicles fully descended into the scrotum. Often, it is difficult to determine this with puppies of two months.

If any doubt exists, then veterinary opinion should be sought, for a cryptorchid (one without testicles in the scrotum) and a monorchid (a dog with only one testicle) are useless to the intending breeder and exhibitor. In Britain and the U.S., dogs with these deficiencies are barred from the show ring.

It is well when buying a female with the intention of breeding her, to check on the mothering ability of her dam. This may not be easy to do, but a few tactful enquiries may prove fruitful. If you intend to breed your own female when she comes of age, it is important to know how her dam bore her. If the mother was a poor one, this tendency might well have been passed on to her daughter, and you will have to cope with it. It is a bad failing and a poor mother can prove a sad worry and expense and, in fact, should not be bred. Try and select a bitch that is feminine, not "doggy" in appearance, for her kind is likely to bear coarse stock. Make sure too that she is structurally ideal for breeding; she will need substance, a nice length of loin and a good wide pelvis. Her intrinsic soundness will be shown by the free, easy gait of the typical Beagle.

Registration

You have a right to expect when you buy your puppy that its pedigree and registration papers should be ready for you to take away with the youngster. The vendor may give you a signed pedigree going back through at least three generations of your puppy's forebears. It should be ascertained that both the sire and dam of your puppy are registered with a recognized Kennel Club. The largest and most prestigious in the United States is the American Kennel Club. If either or both parents are not registered you will not be able to register your own dog until they are, and it often becomes difficult to register mature animals if their papers are not in good order. Therefore, to save trouble later on, it is better to insist on having your puppy registered by the breeder or dealer from whom you purchase it. Sometimes, owing to the time involved between actual application for a registered name and the delivery of the relevant papers by the Club concerned, it may not be possible for the vendor to give you these papers when you take your puppy home. If this happens, the seller should at least give you the names of the sire and dam of the puppy, also their registration numbers, the date of the puppy's birth, and the name of the breeder. You should also secure from the vendor a written guarantee that he will deliver the authentic papers as soon as they come to him. Remember, that a pedigree alone is of no use to you without registration papers.

If you fortunate enough to acquire a lovely Beagle and in later months want to exhibit it and if it is not registered correctly, then exhibition at a properly licensed show is impossible. Also the puppies you breed from an unregistered Beagle cannot themselves be registered.

The system of registration is somewhat different at the American Kennel Club and The Kennel Club in England.

In the United States

The American Kennel Club's method is to supply blue registration application forms to the breeder when he applies to register his litter. There is one for each puppy and on each form the breeder enters the puppy's sex and color, etc., as well as the name of the person to whom he has sold it. If you are the first purchaser, your name will appear on the reverse of the form. However, if the breeder has sold the puppy to someone else first, a pet shop, for instance, then that person has to complete a gray transfer form. Each succeeding owner must do this to ensure that the puppy or dog is registered as his property. When completing the blue form of registration the owner has to select two names for his puppy. This is necessary in case one of the names proves unsuitable in the eyes of the AKC. If both are deemed unsuitable, then the owner will be asked to submit other names. The owner's signature is then appended in Section B of the form and it is forwarded to the AKC with the required fee.

If your puppy has already been registered, the vendor will enter your name and address on the transfer section on the back, and sign it.

In England

The Kennel Club has a Form 1A (for the registration of one dog) or Form 1B (for the registration of more than one dog from the *same* litter). On these forms, fill in the breed, sex, color markings, date of birth, names of sire and dam, their K.C. registration numbers and the names only of the grandparents. Further, the names and addresses of the sire's owner and the dam owner (who would be the breeder of the puppy) are required. A signature from the breeder is required on the form confirming the authenticity of the entered details. The form thus completed, with signature, is usually given to the purchaser of the puppy at time of purchase – unless the form has already been used by the vendor to register the puppy in advance. Should this be the case, then the buyer will be given the Registration Certificate, which is a small semi-stiff card showing the animal's registered name and number.

If the new owner merely takes possession of Form 1A then he will have to enter on it a selection of four names which appeal to him for registration, enter his name and address as new owner, sign the form at the bottom and submit it with the required fee to the Kennel Club. In due course, the Registration Certificate already referred to will be mailed.

Alternatively, if he has bought a puppy already registered and the seller has given him the certificate, then he will need to transfer details of ownership. For this, The Kennel Club has a Form 2 (Transfer Form). On this is entered the animal's registered name and number as well as its breed or variety. On the left hand side appears the current owner's name and address (i.e., the breeder or vendor usually) and on the right side the transferee's name and address. Both party's signatures should appear below their addresses, also the date of the transfer of ownership. This is then forwarded to The Kennel Club with a fee. Later when the transfer has been made, the new owner will receive a Transfer Certificate, which is a buff colored card.

Dogs which are shipped from Great Britain require special "Export Pedigrees" if they are to be eligible for registration in another country. These must be arranged for before the dog leaves the country of origin.

From all the foregoing details on registration and transfer it will be apparent that in whichever country you live, it is important that these matters be dealt with at the time you buy your puppy. Too many purchasers, taken up at the time of new ownership with the joy of the puppy, give scant thought to documentation. Later, when they realize the necessity of official paperwork, registration can develop into a troublesome process, especially if forms have been mislaid, vendors' names have been forgotten, or if they are dead. Duplicate forms in such cases are often difficult, if not impossible, to secure.

SALLY ANNE THOMPSON

The small puppy must feel very bewildered when he is taken away from his litter-mates and brought into unfamiliar surroundings, different people, strange scents and noises, and probably more handling than he has been accustomed to.

V The New Puppy

Bringing the Puppy Home

Having selected your Beagle puppy, your next step is to plan his life for him! A small puppy must feel very bewildered when he is taken away from his littermates and brought into unfamiliar surroundings, different people, strange scents and noises, and probably more handling than he has been accustomed to. It is up to you to reassure him as much as possible for these are days in the youngster's life which may well prove critical in the development of his character.

Car Travel

Car travel may be the first strange thing that happens to the puppy when he leaves the nest. Consequently, the new owner must try and make this rather frightening event one of little importance from the dog's point of view. It is probable that the breeder, knowing your visit indicated a likely sale, deferred feeding the litter until you had made your choice. If he has, it is good, for with an empty stomach the puppy is less likely to be sick on the journey home. Nevertheless, you should be prepared with an old blanket or two, a towel, and some newspapers to cope with the mess if he does become car sick. It is the unusual vibration which upsets the canine stomach and causes nausea. Of course, your puppy will get used to it gradually and, eventually, no doubt, come to love car travel. Most dogs do. The initial stages, however, need to be watched, for if a puppy becomes sick in his early travels he may well develop a complex about cars and vomiting. He may think that every time he enters a car he *has* to be sick! This is a reaction to be avoided and here common sense must prevail. It is wise to have a carton or empty carrier with you just in case you need to put the puppy in it, but try to keep him on your lap, so wear old clothes. If you are driving, it will be necessary to take a companion to act as custodian until you get home.

Back Home

No doubt you will have made adequate preparations for the puppy's arrival. This should include not only his sleeping quarters and his feeding, but apprising the other members of the family circle that a dog is on his way. No animal should be brought into a home unless everyone who lives there is ready to accept it.

It is particularly important that the woman of the house approves. She is usually the one at home most of the time and on her shoulders will fall the task of feeding and caring properly for the little thing. Without her loving care and cooperation your Beagle is unlikely to thrive.

The next thing to consider is where the puppy will sleep. Most one dog owners keep their pets indoors and this is the best place. A lone dog (unless he is strictly a guard dog for the house or property) is not much use out of doors. He learns faster, makes a better home guard and speedily becomes a member of the family when he lives and feeds under the same roof.

The kitchen is the usual place for new puppies, but you may prefer to keep yours in a warm outbuilding or lean-to. Other owners prefer facilities like a well ventilated closet under the stairs, but warmth and complete freedom from drafts are the two main essentials. Introduce the dog to his new quarters at once for he may well want to take a short nap after all the excitement of the day. Puppies, like small children, are asleep more than they are awake, and this should be encouraged. Newspapers should be spread around the bed area; this will encourage the puppy to leave his bed for his natural functions, and, at the same time, allow you to clean up speedily after him. Most puppies will leave their bed when they want to relieve themselves; only a few will soil their bedding. Those that do can often be broken of the habit by actually feeding them on their beds. Instinctively, a good dog will wish to completely dissociate the two functions, and a point in training will have been achieved.

Puppies, like small children, are asleep more than they are awake, and rest should be encouraged. Awake time is play time, a chance to exercise and develop growing skills, strength and coordination.

LOUISE VAN DER MEID

The Bed

These days, there is a wide choice of beds for dogs on the market. One can select from a variety of wicker baskets, square, oblong, or circular, with or without canopies, and of a size to suit the individual breeds at maturity. Alternatively, there are beds which are collapsible, with metal frame work and screened with canvas or cloth in a variety of colors and designs. A visit to your local pet shop or variety store, or a scan through the mail order catalog will find the type you want. Whatever the kind of bed purchased, make sure it is raised from the ground. Even if the room in which your puppy sleeps is draft proof, the added security from under door draft is important in keeping him healthy. In an emergency the Beagle puppy will make do with a nice, comfortable box raised off the floor, and with a doorway cut out half way down one side through which he can enter and leave at will. Collapsible metal beds are very good and are preferable to wicker baskets which may be chewed by the young puppy at teething time, a habit which should be discouraged early. Some risk exists, for chewed pieces are likely to be swallowed and cause distress.

At Night

It is likely that your puppy will cry for the first few nights. He will miss his brothers and sisters and, feeling deserted, will call for them. Do not worry about it. If you have ear plugs, put them in your ears and settle down for the night! The big mistake is to get up to comfort the puppy and take him into your own bed.To ignore him might appear heartless advice, but any experienced breeder will tell you it is the best way to deal with the matter. Your puppy will soon become resigned to his new existence – this seldom takes more than three days, and the nights will then pass in peace.

However, you should do all you can before bed time to reassure the lonely puppy. Some owners use a hot water bottle, covered with a blanket to protect the puppy from the hotness and to protect *it* from the puppy's sharp teeth. An alternative is to put into the bed with the puppy an old stuffed sock about the same size as himself. He will accept this as a companion and rest his head upon it as puppies do when they are in the litter, and this will give him some reassurance. His bed, whether it be box, basket or one of fancy style, should be well padded with a comfortable blanket or sack, for warmth will induce sleep and help the youngster to adjust quickly.

It is often amazing to see what a tranquilizing effect a loudly ticking alarm clock wrapped in a towel and placed in the puppy's bed can have on him. You may have to leave it there every night for a week, until he has become "at home".

Puppy Feeding

How you feed your new puppy is a matter of common sense. If you have children and have reared them well and they are healthy, then apply the same principles to your dog. The process is the same even if the shapes differ! Your puppy should be completely independent from his mother even if you acquire him at six or seven weeks of age. In fact, he should not have seen her for at least a week prior to that age.

At six weeks he should be on three milky meals, and two or three meat meals. The breeder should give you a diet sheet indicating the times, type and quantity of the feeding, and this you should follow from the moment you bring your puppy home. The idea of so many meals a day is to avoid distention of the stomach muscles. What it really amounts to is that you have one adequate milky meal and one adequate meat meal, but you split each of these into three parts and alternate them, milky meal, meat meal, milky meal, and so on, making six separate feedings. The puppy, having a small stomach, assimilates these small meals easily and gets maximum nutrition from them. If you give him a lot at once you will cause him to swell up like a balloon, stretching his stomach muscles to a dangerous extent, and giving him dyspepsia. The food should be supplemented with vitamins, calcium and Vitamin D, all important at this stage. There are proprietary additives available on the market and these should be used, but in moderation. The value of vitamins is well known and these are dealt with separately in this book. A suggested menu for the new Beagle puppy about two months old is as follows:

Milky Meal – 3 to 6 tablespoons warm milk
2 to 3 tablespoons baby cereal or commercial puppy food.
Meat Meal – 2 to 4 heaping teaspoons raw ground meat.

SALLY ANNE THOMPSON

It should be remembered that the correct feeding of your puppy can make all the difference between winning or not winning in the show ring. If a dog is healthy he will look forward to mealtimes.

These should be alternated approximately every three hours throughout the day. In one of the feedings include ½ to 1 teaspoon of cod liver oil and a puppy vitamin and mineral supplement according to the directions on the container.

As the puppy grows older, the number of meals can be reduced but the quantity should be gradually increased. You may find he will omit some meals himself, those between midday and six o'clock usually coming into disfavor. As soon as this happens, do not attempt to coax him to eat; just eliminate that meal from the schedule. This reduction in mealtimes can continue until the puppy is about nine months old. By then he should be on two meals a day, a light one of a little meat and some kibbled meal before midday, with a substantial raw meat meal in the evening. When he reaches his "hound-hood" he can be fed one meal a day. Details of this one big meal will be given later.

It should be remembered that correct feeding of your puppy can make all the difference between winning or not winning in the show ring. A well-bred Beagle can survive and look good on an average diet but on an excellent diet and good care he will look even better. This is a point often overlooked by those owners who do not realize that in puppy feeding economy is no virtue.

Care should be taken in the matter of bones. Many bones, particularly those of rabbit, fish or poultry, are dangerous. The best bone is the big beef knuckle or marrow bone. These make for a good gnaw, and constitute no danger because they will not splinter. The puppy with the doubtful mouth – that is, one which tends to be undershot – should never be allowed bones, at least not until final dentition, for the action of bone-biting may only aggravate the condition.

A small hanging door, hinged to swing back and forth, is easy to construct, and allows your dog to enter and leave at will.

PURINA PET CARE CENTER

Commercial Food

Perhaps the best advice on the question of puppy diet is to leave it to your veterinarian. If you prefer to do without his services, then consider one of the best available puppy foods on the market and follow the directions on the container. Some of these foods have had long years of research behind them and often do a better job of growing puppies than any diet you are likely to concoct yourself.

A good rule of thumb for rapid growth is to feed all the puppy can eat three times a day until he is three months old, drop to two meals a day until he is full grown, which should be at six months if the diet has been adequate. If he appears to have swallowed a croquet ball due to his stretched stomach, that does him no harm.

You can find elaborate schedules for feeding puppies. Follow them if that gives you pleasure, but they are almost always two or three times as costly as a sound commercial puppy food, and no better in the end.

Handling the Puppy

Some puppies are grossly over-handled, especially by children. They should be told that a dog has four feet and those four feet are made to go on the ground! No puppy likes to be grabbed up into human arms all day long. It is boring. He would rather be exploring the place and savoring the smells which all pups love; the way some people lift dogs requires a lot of tolerance on their pet's part.

Small puppies straight from the nest are often lifted by the scruffs of their necks. The scruff is a looseness of skin which covers the crest or upper part of the neck and it is this the dam takes gently between her jaws when she wishes to transport one of her puppies from one place to another. It is a safe method when the puppies are very small and light. However, once they have taken on some size and weight, this way of lifting is uncomfortable, even painful. The best way to lift a puppy of, say ten weeks, is to put one hand under its chest between the forelegs, the other hand behind the elbow, also under the chest; the hands will then be at right angles to each other, with his hind legs tucked under your elbow. Steady the puppy against your chest and, in this position, he will be secure and unable to wriggle or jump to the ground as puppies sometimes do when

SALLY ANNE THOMPSON

Care should be taken to see that the small puppy (or adult dog, for that matter) is not teased. Thoughtless harassment often plays havoc with a dog's temperament.

they get bored. Never pick up, or allow a puppy to be picked up by the forelegs. Not only does it hurt the puppy, it can throw out a youngster's shoulders and spoil him for exhibiton work.

What to Avoid

There are a number of things to avoid with a small puppy. One of them is overfeeding. Many Beagles are greedy and will eat *ad infinitum* if allowed. Avoid foods that are greasy or spicy. Never feed candy – milk chocolate is fattening and unsuited to dogs.

Do not overtire a puppy. This applies not only to too much exercise, but also to play around the home. Children are the main offenders in this respect. They do not realize the limited powers of endurance possessed by a young puppy needing plenty of sleep between his short playtime intervals, and especially after meals.

Care should be taken to see that the small puppy (or adult dog for that matter) is not teased. Thoughtless harassment often plays havoc with a dog's temperament. Even the best of dogs can come to the end of his tether, and retaliate with a bite. When this happens he is at once damned as vicious and, through no fault of his own, poor chap, is either given away or destroyed. Never leave a small puppy alone for long periods. A youngster needs company, either of his own kind or of his family. Left to his own devices, not only can he get into mischief (such as chewing furniture or ripping up floor-coverings) for which he will get punished out of hand, but also the silence and the misery of his isolated state will spoil his temperament. Avoid tying up a puppy and leaving him alone. He will rebel at once against restraint and either get tangled up in the rope or leash and strangle himself, or the confinement will render him sullen. If the Beagle has to be taught to live at the end of a chain (let us hope not) train him to it by easy stages so that, in time, he will come to accept it without question. This type of training, however, should not be started until the puppy is at least five months old.

Outdoor Kenneling

The Beagle is, of course, singularly adapted to outdoor living. Being a hound, his forebears lived this way and the average Beagle will not turn a hair if he is asked to live in a kennel. If you keep a number of dogs, then there is no other way of housing them.

There are a number of excellent ready-built kennels on the market and your choice can be made from a wide range depending on your pocketbook and the number of dogs you want to maintain. For the small breeding kennel, perhaps with three bitches and a male, some cleverly designed houses are available. These have separate compartments of suitable size to keep a Beagle comfortable, and have a sleeping bench raised out of the way of drafts.

Make sure too that you have an isolation kennel away from the main one, just in case you ever have a sick animal. It is a good idea to arrange a detached place where straw bedding can be stored and kennel equipment kept, handy for morning work in the runs. The whole setup should be surrounded by strong chain link fencing. It is better if each kennel compartment has its own individual run.

The kennel itself should be at least six feet high to enable the owner to stand inside with comfort. The site should be carefully chosen. It should be well drained and, for this, gravel or sandy soil is best. A south or southwest exposure is ideal. Make sure that the kennel is sheltered from bad weather, yet allowing ample sunlight and fresh air to filter through. Trees make a good screen, but care should be taken to see that the kennels are not overhung with foliage in the summer.

The floor and the runs should be made of concrete and the kennels raised entirely on brick, the gap between the ground and the kennel floor being filled in all around to keep your dogs from crawling underneath, and to keep out trespassing vermin. The woodwork should be impregnated with a preservative harmless to dogs. If this is done three or four times a year such a kennel will last for many generations of dogs.

The sleeping benches, which should slide out or be detachable in some way for easy cleaning, should be treated with linseed oil at frequent intervals. Lead-based paint or any wood treatment containing lead should never be used since many dogs lick it and become sick. The essence of success with such a kennel, whether it be modest or elaborate, is cleanliness. Hygiene is vitally important; it cannot be stressed enough. Attention should be given daily to the dogs' comfort. Used sawdust, excelsior, straw or other bedding should be burnt. Disinfecting is a daily task for the conscientious owner and there are some first-class dog preparations for doing this on the market today, although some household disinfectants are also effective.

The color you paint your doghouse has a great influence on the inside temperature. On a sunny summer day a white house can be as much as 20° cooler.

PURINA PET CARE CENTER

SALLY ANNE THOMPSON

How you handle your puppy when he first arrives will be the basis for the relationship between the two of you for the rest of his life. Good food, clean quarters, firm yet gentle discipline, and most of all, love!

Every kennel would be better if a Vapona bar were hung in it, or if large, one bar to every 1000 cubic feet of space. The vapor which it gives off destroys fleas and lice as well as many other species of insects found in kennels. Flies and mosquitoes are also killed. By killing mosquitoes the bar helps to prevent the spread of heartworm.

If your new puppy has always been kept indoors, it is wise to keep him inside with you a short while before introducing him to the kennel. This applies especially if he has come to you in bleak weather for a drastic change in living conditions will do him no good. However, if the season is fair and he is to be a kennel dog, the sooner he starts living outdoors the better. Otherwise, he may find it difficult to adjust to kennel life once he has enjoyed the coziness of indoor existence.

SALLY ANNE THOMPSON

An ill-mannered dog reflects unfavorably on the training ability of his owner, so it behooves you to instill sound tractability in your Beagle. He is so cute, and at this age he does so little harm that it is difficult to reprimand him. As he grows older it will quickly become apparent that a firmer hand is needed to keep him in order.

VI Good Habits - - - And Bad

An ill-mannered dog reflects unfavorably on the training ability of his owner, so it behooves you to instill sound tractability in your Beagle. It is easy enough to forego early training when you see your puppy playing around the home, mischievous perhaps, but with all his cheekiness doing little harm. At such an age he is quite easy to control, but as he grows older it will quickly become apparent that a firmer hand is needed to keep him in order. The methods employed in achieving a puppy's training are simple enough, based as they are on sound and kindly common sense principles. If these are applied patiently and regularly, quick results will be your reward.

Learning His Name

As soon as you get your puppy, give him a name. Certain names suit certain dogs and it is all right to wait a day or two before deciding. But don't delay too long, as many new owners do, trying to make up their minds, because the earlier a puppy learns his name, the better. A short, sharp name is best – a monosyllable, or at most one with two syllables, to make for terse calling.

Use his name constantly in elementary training, call him by name frequently – and always to meals – and when he responds, reward him with a tidbit. It is most important for a dog to know his name as it is more difficult to exercise control over one who does not.

Housebreaking

The first lesson to be taught your new puppy is house cleanliness. The length of time this takes varies from breed to breed, dog to dog, owner to owner. The Beagle is comparatively easy to train in this essential to happy home life, and a puppy, say two months old, should be seeking the yard or kitchen door to go outside after only a few days of persistent training. If you live in an apartment or a home without a yard you will have to train your Beagle to use either layers of newspaper or cat litter. Most Beagles are naturally clean and will never dirty their beds. If the sleeping place is surrounded with spread newspapers the puppy will usually relieve himself on the paper, for his instinctive cleanliness will direct him to do so. Should he stray, however, beyond the confines of the paper or tray provided and leave a puddle on the carpet, it will do no good to scold or slap him. You must catch him just as he is squatting. Put him back on the paper and speak to him kindly when he voids there.

The instant a puppy opens his eyes after sleep he will want to urinate. At this point keep your eyes upon him. He will rise, stretch, leave the bed and start to wander. At any moment he will squat and urinate. If he appears to be straying beyond his legimate confines, he must be eased, maybe prodded back. He will give up at last and then urinate. When he has done this on the paper or litter tray, he should be praised and fussed over. He will speedily learn where to relieve himself! If you fail to correct his mistakes at the time you can hardly blame the puppy. You must certainly never scold him on these occasions for he will not know why you are upset. With a puppy urination is frequent, although in quite small quantities. Evacuation normally occurs four or five times a day in a healthy youngster. For housebreaking purposes, after-meal times should be watchful moments for the trainer, although the efficient tutor will keep his eyes "skinned" constantly.

If you have a yard where the puppy can relieve himself you are fortunate. The paper-trained youngster can be brought near to the yard door by the gradual shifting of newspaper from his bedside to a position close to the door. Soon the paper can be moved into the yard itself and a few days of this will have the puppy well trained. It helps, of course, if the training can be done in clement summer months. Much faster results can then be achieved. In bad weather it could prove fatal to keep a small puppy outdoors for too long.

Some owners have developed a faster method of training the pup to relieve himself outdoors. Bearing in mind that all puppies urinate

SALLY ANNE THOMPSON

If you have a yard you are fortunate. Here you can housebreak the dog, romp with him and train him under the most favorable conditions.

on waking, they keep a close eye on the trainee while he is asleep. The instant he opens his eyes, he is picked up, and, almost ceremonially, taken to the outside door, the door opened, and the puppy is placed outdoors and a word of command given. The word can be anything apt. Many trainers say merely "Outside," some say "Garden". In fact, it does not matter what the word is so long as it is short and clear. The exercise should be repeated many times and before long it will be found that the puppy commences a trek to the outer door the instant he gets the word. Soon, even the word will be unnecessary. If he makes a mistake in your presence, pick him up and take him to the offending spot on the floor. Hold him near to it, scold him and apply a sharp slap to his rear end. Then utter the word of command as you deposit him outside, closing the door in his face. He will not like this treatment at all and the facts of life will soon begin to register. Discipline should be applied only at the time of the misdemeanor; it will have no effect if you delay scolding until some hours later. The memory of a puppy is short and, because of this, it is unfair to chastise him for something he has already forgotten.

It is important to wipe over the offending spots at once with a rag which has been dampened with a strong disinfecting fluid, or with ammonia or vinegar. This will deodorize the area so that the puppy will not be attracted back to make further messes.

Curb Training

While he is out on leash he will want to relieve himself and you should take this opportunity to give him curb training. No dog should be allowed to foul the sidewalk; teach him to evacuate in the gutter. It is reasonably simple to edge your dog to the curb when his movement is imminent, and after a few lessons he will always go to the gutter when he wants to evacuate.

The same rule applies to the dog's urination, although this is more difficult. The female can be taught to use the gutter since she squats when she urinates, but the male, with the approach of puberty, raises his leg and directs a stream wherever he wishes to leave his mark. This heritage from the wild state once acted as a trail setter and territory marker. Unfortunately, the male who dispenses his urine in small doses over a wide area is often responsible for ruining valuable shrubs, soiling cars, shop fronts and in less pleasing

SALLY ANNE THOMPSON

Affix the leash and attempt to get the puppy to walk along with you in an easy manner. With some encouragement and cajolery he will soon quiet down and become an orderly pupil.

cases, bystanders legs. To minimize the dogs' opportunities for this unpleasantness you can do little except endeavor to anticipate the raising of his leg! A good plan is to train him to use one or two spots where his urination can cause no offence. Once he had adopted such places he will invariably save up for them.

Leash Training

The ideal time to commence leash training is when the puppy is about three months old. Initial practice can begin in the yard or the house. By this time he will have received his immunization shots so it should be safe to take him out. Buy him a cheap, narrow strap collar and a leash to match. Put the collar on him for short periods throughout the day. He will probably object to it, and your common sense should guide you as to how long to leave it on.

Affix the leash and attempt to get the puppy to walk along with you in an easy manner. It is unlikely that you will achieve this at first; the youngster will act more like a trout on the end of a line than a dog on a leash. However, with some encouragement and cajolery he will soon quiet down and become an orderly pupil. You should endeavor to get him to walk at your side, leash slack, in an easy gait without pulling or dragging. If he pulls ahead, give the lead a sharp jerk to stop him. If he holds back, drag him forward a little, or the attraction of a tidbit may bring him to you. He will find that it is much more comfortable and sensible to conform rather than to suffer a sore neck from pulling, or sore pads from dragging. Try and use the command "Heel" when you pull him back level with your left leg. It is a useful command, one that seems to be readily understood by dogs.

The persistent puller can be cured if you carry a rolled up newspaper with you when you walk him. When he rushes forward not heeding the command "Heel", snap the newspaper to his nose and repeat the command. The noise made by the paper coupled with its harmless impact will prove effective in bringing him to heel, and once this has been achieved the mere showing of the baton will suffice.

After your puppy is walking nicely, and when he is a little older, a choke chain can be substituted for the leather collar. This will hang comfortably around his neck like a necklace, and can be tightened when he gets out of line.

Exercise

This is a most important factor in the rearing of your dog. When you have him housetrained and leash-trained, he can then be given exercise out of doors, and you will feel safe knowing that he will behave well in public.

Exercise should be given at regular intervals. The dog enjoys anticipating his walk. He can tell almost to the second when he will be taken out. Admittedly, this uncanny ability is frequently an irritation, even an embarrassment to the fondest owner. Sometimes the weather outside is bad, it is pouring rain, or snow, or maybe you are just exhausted from your day at the office. Just the same, the dog wants to go out and his entreaty, sometimes accompanied by barking, leaves you in no doubt as to what you must do! So out you go! You will find that your dog benefits from these time clock outings and his natural functions will be geared to fit them.

It should be remembered that although your Beagle is a hound and used to running free in work, you will achieve best results toward muscling him and forming his body nicely by *walking* him. Never use a harness, for this does not suit the Beagle. Keep him on collar and leash for long distances, certainly for several miles a day; such hiking will do you good too, no doubt! Get over as much rough ground as you can find. Stony terrain, or cinder tracks are excellent, for these will harden and strengthen the Beagle's feet and pasterns as well as build up his hindquarters.

Let him loose at times, of course, but not in places where danger lurks from passing traffic. Keep a close eye on his loins and as soon as you note any signs of thickness there, give him more exercise to work off the fat, for a fat Beagle is an abhorrence. An occasional game with a ball will prove beneficial and this is best played on parkland or open space. If you can throw the ball up an incline and have the Beagle race after it, this will prove a great hindquarter exercise and your dog will enjoy the game of retrieving.

Keeping Off Furniture

You will probably find that following your training in house cleanliness, walking, and the usual elementary matters, your Beagle will prove quite "biddable". This means that he will be trained to accept, more or less, the word of command. It is important then, that he be taught where he can go in the house and which places are forbidden. It is not uncommon for a dog to plant himself on particularly choice comfort spots like armchairs, beds, and sofas. Some dogs even hog the hearth denying its heat to the family members. With the advent of central heating, perhaps this last habit creates no annoyance, but no one wants to find a dog in possession of his

SALLY ANNE THOMPSON

An occasional game of ball is ideal to work off some of the fat which may accumulate when a Beagle is under-exercised.

favorite chair. Get on to the Beagle right from the start. When he jumps up on the chair or bed and takes over, push him off. Use the word "No" with considerable emphasis and guide him to the place where you want him to rest. Maybe a special slip-mat or rug can be arranged for him to relax on. After you have ushered him from the wrong place to the right place a few times he will have caught on to your wishes. If he is incorrigible and you need a firmer approach to achieve your wishes, utilize the newspaper baton, already referred to. A sharp "No" together with a crack from the rolled-up newspaper has its effect on many dogs. If you cannot lay your hand on the baton, then toss a book or magazine just close enough to miss him. This will startle him off the chair or bed. Most dogs view the human ability to throw with great respect. They find it something they cannot easily retaliate against, and this kind of action usually wins the day.

Chewing

When the puppy is teething, usually between three and five months of age, he has a propensity to chew or gnaw on anything which comes his way. Far better to wait until the teething problem is over before expensive equipment is bought. It is also a habit of youngsters to test the value of their jaws on anything and everything. Bearing this in mind, make sure that you leave nothing about on which the puppy can chew. It is not uncommon for owners to complain that their fine slippers have been torn up, their expensive rugs ruined and so on. Irritating as such things can be, *it is more the fault of the owner for leaving the things there for the puppy to chew than that of the puppy himself.*

In most cases a cure can be effected by finding the dog an alternative to chew on. There are a number of toys on the market, the most popular, perhaps, being a hard rubber bone, and if you can wean him over to this – or even a good marrow bone – not only will he prefer it, he is more likely to overlook your household treasures. It should be remembered that whenever a puppy is caught doing anything of which you disapprove, he should be instantly reprimanded. This scolding should be quite severe. Mild admonishments have little effect, for the dog will learn only by being made to feel contrite, or to feel pain.

If the chewing habit appears chronic, you may have to resort to daubing the favored articles with a strong solution of bitter aloes or one of the special repellent sprays which are marketed for this purpose.

Jumping On People

Nothing exhibits the badly trained animal worse than the dog that bounds all over visitors, and shows his exuberance in public places to complete strangers, dirtying their clothes with his muddy paws and making a nuisance of himself. This failing needs rectifying immediately so when he jumps, push him firmly away from you with the command, "Down." If he is persistent, tread on his back paws as you give the command. If this does not work, then anticipate his jump by flexing your knee. He will bump into it as he comes up and be thrown backwards. A few lessons like this will help to cure him, providing you use the word "No" every time.

SALLY ANNE THOMPSON

If you are to exercise control over your dog he must learn to respond when his name is called. With a long, light leash attached to his collar coax and tug him to you, repeating his name frequently. Entice him with a tidbit.

Some indication as to whether your training has had effect can be had by getting a friend to walk in; probably the dog will bound towards him. Order, "No", and you should see some results, either a complete stay in the dog's rush or at least a faltering. You will then know how much firmness to apply for optimum results.

Needless Barking

A yapping puppy and a barking dog constitute a nuisance to your neighbors. It is well to commence training your young barker at once, otherwise the complaints from people nearby will bring the law upon you with an injunction to either quiet or dispose of him. Much of the training needed to eradicate this bad habit takes psychological form.

First, it is better to keep the offender in a small room than in a spacious one. In this he may feel more cozy and it will give him a sense of security. When you leave the house, linger outside for a time, making sure that the dog with his keen hearing cannot detect your presence. As soon as he starts to bark, creep back and bang on the door, shouting, "Quiet" or "No", a word which he should have become used to by now. A silence will ensue from within. This may be only momentary, followed at once by more barking. Again bang on the door, shouting at him. He will be surprised at this, and his silence this time will last longer.

If he persists, bang open the door, take him by the collar and whack him with the newspaper baton shouting, "Quiet" or "No", or the command you have decided to use. He will not like this at all, and the chances are that he will now settle down quietly for quite a while. You, on your part, have to be patient, and this means that in spite of the protracted silence you will have to wait silently outside the door. The very moment a whimper or a bark is heard be ready with a raised hand to thump on the door. The method is a sort of shock treatment which often pays off with dogs of average intelligence.

However, there are some dogs that appear quite stubborn and cannot be silenced, regardless of what is done to them. In fact, a good walloping seems to incite them to greater use of their lungs. These dogs present a problem and demand much stronger action. You will have to act as though you are in a very bad temper. Of course, you may well be in one by the time you have had to chastise him half-a-dozen times! Have a loaded water pistol ready to squirt into his face when you open the door. If the dog is in a spot where water can do no damage, a cupful thrown at him will act as a deterrent. The thing to do is to get him to associate the opening of his mouth to bark with some unpleasant result. Once this has sunk into his consciousness he will be loath to start up for fear of what may happen. If he barks in your presence, seize his muzzle, hold the jaws together with one hand while you slap him across the rump with the other, the command "No" being repeated all the time.

If such painless treatment fails, then when he barks pick him up by the scruff of the neck and the skin on the back and shake him so hard that his teeth all but fall out. There is no better way of showing your displeasure.

The danger exists, of course, that when a dog has been broken of careless barking, he may be silent at a time when barking is needed, i.e., when intruders threaten. This is a chance you will have to

SALLY ANNE THOMPSON

This puppy is only 6 months old, but already he is being taught to stand correctly for the show ring.

take since, obviously, you must break him of this bad habit. However, most dogs, even after correction, will prove intelligent enough to know when their barking is required and when it is not, so the point need not worry you unduly.

If you are interested in your dog's acting as an alarm, allow him a few barks, before commanding "Quiet". In this manner you can control him, and turn a vice into a useful virtue.

Car Chasing

This is a very bad habit, one not easy to break. A lot of dogs get killed and frequently endanger the lives of motorists. Unfortunately, some owners seem to view car chasing as an amusing habit and do nothing to break it when, for the dog's own safety, it should be checked as soon as noted.

Sometimes, a good trouncing at the time will help, but training needs to be carried through persistently until the dog is quite resigned to not chasing cars.

A good plan is to arrange with a friend to drive along your street in his automobile, and as soon as your dog attacks the moving vehicle, to slow up, lean out of the window, and squirt some unpleasant fluid straight in his face. A few lessons like this should have desired effect, but, in any case, dogs with this bad habit should never be allowed out unattended.

General Hints

The important thing is never to let your puppy cultivate any habit which is likely to become an annoyance later no matter how amusing it might seem at the time. The habit of biting your leg or hand may provoke only laughter when it is done by a two month old Beagle, but when the dog is a year old and still does it, it is far less funny.

Another factor which is too often overlooked in family circle training is that even though you might train the dog effectively, other members of the family, less interested, perhaps, or maybe easier going, will allow him to do things which he would dare not attempt if you were present. It will behoove you, therefore, to instruct the family to follow your example! Make it quite clear that you are going to a great deal of trouble in training the Beagle and that you do not want your work, or the dog, spoiled by lack of their cooperation. Most families will realize the importance of this and cooperate willingly.

Mental Care

A dog will always thrive if he is happy, barring some maladjustment in his heritage. The owner should make sure that his Beagle puppy is brought into a kind and understanding atmosphere. Too many small puppies find themselves in homes where, after the novelty of ownership has worn off, they are subjected to indignities, sometimes even cruelty. A dog needs to feel secure and to have a bond of understanding with his master, and it is up to his master to promote this, for it is the only way to get the best from a dog. Beagles usually enter the world with an equable disposition; they are seldom shy or nervous, and those grown dogs that are usually owe it to some human mistreatment. It is important that a puppy always knows what is expected of him. He must learn to recognize your authority, and if you apply it sensibly he will come to respect you.

Remember that when a dog wants to sleep he should be left alone. If children are about, it should be made clear that the puppy is not to be disturbed. Children are often the cause of indifferent temperament in a dog. They are inclined to treat the youngster as a toy, and push and prod him about until he is aggravated enough to show his displeasure. Then, unfortunately for the dog, he gets the blame for what is wrongly interpreted as a weak point in his breeding or temperament.

A dog accustomed to human companionship should not be left alone for extended periods. A few hours at a time do him no harm, but a full day of loneliness does little for his peace of mind. He needs human company to be contented and this is his just due. This does not mean that a working couple should not keep a dog! What it does mean is that the puppy must adjust to their schedule, and povision made for his sanitary arrangements. Quite apart from this, a naturally clean dog forced for too long to contain himself because such arrangements have not been made, is likely to develop a kidney condition or worse; such treatment of an animal is tantamount to cruelty.

The happiest dog is the trained one – he understands what is wanted of him and how to go about doing it, enjoying the pleasure he gives his family by his willingness and ability.

Social Behavior

Recent genetic studies emphasize the importance of heredity in the development of dog behavior. Heredity has an important effect on almost every trait tested. This study was by Drs. J. P. Scott and John L. Fuller, working at the Jackson Laboratory, Bar Harbor, Maine. They worked with five breeds of dogs representing the major groups: Wire-Hair Fox Terrier, American Cocker Spaniel, African Basenji, Shetland Sheepdog and the Beagle.

Among other things, they found that sex does have definite effects upon the aggressive tendencies of dogs and upon the dominance order, but not upon their trainability and ability to solve problems. This means then that the male is more dominant (the pack leader) and aggressive, but that the female is his equal when it comes to training and intelligence.

Inherited emotional traits profoundly influence performance. Although the various breeds differed widely in emotional and motivational characteristics, no one breed was superior to any other in solving problems. Detailed statistical analyses indicate that there is a highly complex relationship between the basic genetic inheritance and its final effect upon behavior.

Perhaps the most important of their findings so far as the pet owner is concerned is that there is a critical period in the puppy's life which exerts a lasting influence upon its adult behavior and ability to adjust to human relationships. A puppy removed from its mother and littermates at the age of six to eight weeks, and brought into a home and family environment, where it is handled and petted, has a far better chance of becoming a well-adjusted dog in its relationships with both people and other dogs than the one left behind in the kennel where, although it is adequately fed and housed, it is not given the advantage of human handling. For a puppy to turn out well then, it should be brought into the home as early as possible (before it is eight weeks old) and certainly not after 13 weeks if it has never known the human touch. Let me emphasize that this contact with humans need not necessarily be extensive. Even picking a dog up gently once a day is sufficient to establish the proper rapport.

LOUISE VAN DER MEID

The size of a dog is determined both genetically and by his environment, principally the diet. An undernourished dog may never achieve full size. The two Beagles shown here have been bred to different sizes. One is under 13 inches and the other close to 15. This is genetically determined, a matter of breeding.

VII Feeding

Feeding is a matter of far less complexity than is generally believed. If you were to throw your dog a lump of raw meat every evening at 7 p.m. and made sure that he had fresh water two or more times daily (according to the climate), he would thrive marvellously for a short time but his growth rate would not be maintained on this diet alone, since muscle meat is not a complete food. The average dog owner, however, wants to know more about the intricacies of specialized feeding, vitamin application, and so on. This is a good thing, for it shows that the owner has an interest in his dog's well-being and wants only the best for him.

The Beagle can be a rough eater. By this is meant he can cope with carcasses which have been thrown to him and enjoy them The tastiest parts (and the most nutritious, incidentally) are the liver, brain, spleen, and the intestines.

Paunch and offal feeds are ideal; they build a dog up into excellent condition, and he will enjoy too the process of tearing out his food. However, this method of feeding will hardly meet with general aesthetic approval. Quite apart from the mess involved, a certain amount of antipathy will be experienced in handling carcasses, so most dog owners will prefer the more conventional diets.

An adult Beagle may be maintained on one meal a day from the time he is about nine or ten months old, assuming of course that he is well developed and does not appear to require any special diet. The meal can be fed raw or lightly cooked; there appears little to choose between the benefits of either form, although it would seem that raw meat, provided it is absolutely fresh, has greater

This is the result of an interesting experiment. The two Beagles are litter-mates and were fed exactly the same foods. However, the ingredients fed to the larger, were blended together, while those for the smaller were fed individually so that he could pick and choose according to his taste. The results are obvious, and should be a lesson to those of us who believe that a dog is capable of regulating his own diet.

PURINA PET CARE CENTER

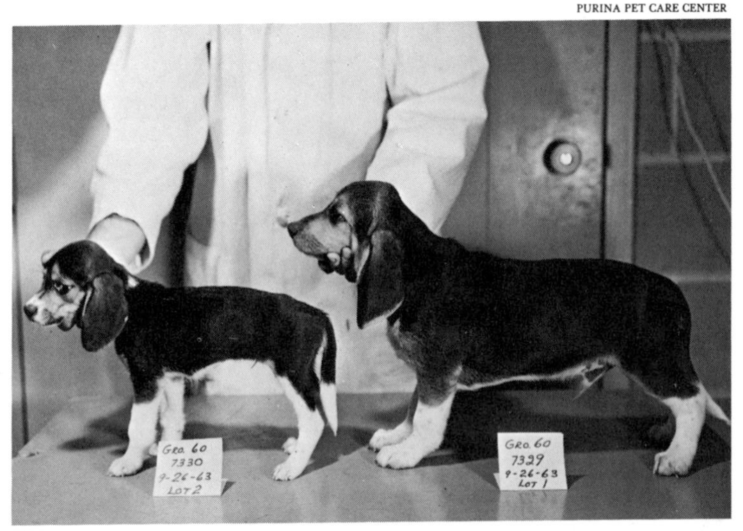

value than cooked. However, most dogs – even those on the conventional one meal a day – are given a lunchtime snack of biscuit meal soaked in a little gravy or milk. This along with the fresh water which must be available at all times will contribute to his need for nutritional moisture.

Dogs, like people, sometimes prefer their food well-presented. Variety too will keep a dog's appetite primed, and this is important if you are the owner of a choosy feeder. Hounds fed in the pack or the litter compete against each other; consequently, members either feed or starve and the indifferent feeder has to show some interest in the meal or go without. The lone dog, however, can please himself. If he is made that way, and some dogs are, and seem to thrive, he will eat only when he is really ravenous and this may be once every two days! Such finicky dogs are usually a worry to their owners. These individuals may need special attention to make sure they are not infested with worms, or have some deficiency which affects their appetite. Only your veterinarian can advise you on this.

Vitamins

Some foods may well lack the specific vitamins needed to complete your dog's diet. Certainly, it has been found that certain canine diseases and conditions are caused through vitamin deficiencies. Vitamin D, essential to the Beagle's good health, may be manufactured in the body by the action of sunlight, or obtained through correct feeding. The shortage of sunlight in some lands and the general unavailability of the right foods suggest a need for a complete vitamin supplement. The best-known vitamins are as follows:

Vitamin A: This is found in heart and liver, fish liver, oils, milk and eggs. It is also found in raw carrots and parsley. It is a good builder of strong bone in puppies and is useful in resisting infection. Believed to support eye health, it is also purported to be a factor preventing a tendency toward night blindness, common in some breeds.

Vitamin B: This is usually referred to as B complex. The vitamins which compose it are found in milk, meat, eggs, liver, wheat germ and yeast. They are particularly good for improving the skin and coat. Dogs of a nervous disposition and poor "do-ers" appear to benefit from it.

Vitamin C: This is known as the "sunshine" vitamin. It is obtained from grass, citrus fruits, and tomatoes. Milk also contains Vitamin C. It is a valuable general vitamin, being essential to growth, good teeth and healthy skin.
Vitamin D: It is found in egg yolk, butter, liver, and the fish oils. In conjunction with vitamin A it is obtained to some extent from cod liver oil and halibut liver oil. It is wise to give it to in-whelp bitches and young stock in conjunction with bonemeal. It aids in the assimilation of calcium and other minerals.
Vitamin E: Found in wheat germ oil. It is necessary for only young puppies.

In summary, then, if you want your dog to enjoy perfect health, he will need ample food in the form of a well-rounded diet. This is found in the better prepared dog foods available in all markets. No raw or cooked meat is essential as was once thought. The individual dog owner cannot prepare his own dog diets as well or as inexpensively as he can buy it in prepared foods, especially in the form of dry foods to which it is necessary only to add water. Adding fat to increase the calories helps to cut expense and too it is benefical as a source of fatty acid.

How to Feed

The best way to feed a Beagle is to place his bowl on a low platform so that he does not have to bend his head too far forward to take the food. This method aids head deportment and although it is not essential to his well-being, it is likely to improve his general appearance,

When to Feed

Obviously, your own convenience should dictate this, but the best time from a dog's viewpoint is to have his main meal in the evening. Some people feed their Beagle, then take him for a walk. This is wrong, for the dog gets less benefit from his food than when he is

Edible fats are important in a dog's diet, particularly if he is to have a smoothy glossy coat like this English Champion, Rossut Vagabond. The stern appears to be dropped slightly due to the photography. ▶

Contrary to popular opinion, big knobby knees do not mean Rickets. As we can see here, Rickets is characterized by soft, easily bent bones. These are the result of feeding either an insufficient or an improper proportion of vitamin D, calcium, and phosphorus.

SALLY ANNE THOMPSON

SALLY ANNE THOMPSON

Feed him all he can hold, three times a day, until he is 4 months old.

fed and bedded down. In the wild, the dog would kill, eat and then rest, and, although we are not dealing with wild ones, the domestic dog reacts the same way.

A good time to feed is in the late evening. One will assume that your Beagle has had a midday snack, at least a saucer of milk during the afternoon. This can only do him good, but his main interest is in the main meal that he has been looking forward to all day. Keep to a regular feeding time so that he knows when to expect food. Regularity in feeding tones up the body, creates a healthy appetite and sets, as a rule, a regular time for the natural functions.

How Much to Feed

The quantity of food to give the puppy and the adult dog is always a source of concern to new owners, for they have no wish to either overfeed or underfeed their pets. A good rule of puppy feeding, say one of two to three months, is to give a quantity that can be squeezed lightly into a ball roughly the size of the puppy's head. This amount should be considered his daily ration and be divided into several portions, according to the number of feedings he has during the day.

Feed him all he can hold three times a day until he is four months old and then twice a day until six to nine months, after which one meal a day is quite enough. Make sure that the mature dog is not overfed. As do humans, dogs thrive better when they finish a meal still feeling a little hungry rather than staggering away replete. Most healthy dogs will eat a third more than they need and store the excess as fat. This is to be avoided.

If you are still in doubt as to how much to feed your dog, give him what seems an adequate quantity. Watch the Beagle eating. He will start off with gusto, then gradually ease off as he becomes replete. At some point (if he has too much) he will come up for air, and it can be safely assumed that he has had enough. However, the test should be made for three days running, and the quantity left on each occasion averaged and omitted from future meals.

PURINA PET CARE CENTER

An adequate, well-balanced diet is essential if you want your pet to have the playful vigor we see here.

SALLY ANNE THOMPSON

When puppies are being weaned it is best to separate their meals from the mother's while feeding.

What food is left should be removed at once. Never leave it down in the hope that the dog will come back and finish it. When Beagles are hungry they will not discriminate in what they eat, and stale food or food unpleasantly fouled by flies or vermin can only do them harm.

What to Avoid

Never feed sloppy meals. These lack nutrient value. Avoid foods from the family table which have been garnished with strong sauces. Your Beagle might enjoy the occasional meal of Spaghetti Neapolitan, but to include it regularly on his menu may mean you will have an over-fat and loose-boweled dog on your hands. Simple feeding *must* be the rule for dogs and, although they may have to exist on leftovers from the family table, care should be taken to ensure that the dog's bowl does not contain wrong foods, nor foods which contain preservative chemicals. Currants and raisins do not suit the canine stomach and sweets (candies) should be given sparingly. This does not, of course, mean the commercially prepared dog "candies" which are highly nutritious.

Commercial Foods

Today these are many and varied. Most of them are extremely well-prepared, the many manufacturers of human foods having come to realize the vast amount of business to be done with dog owners. Frozen foods and packaged foods are available in abundance and a glance through the Pet Foods Department of your supermarket or the window of your nearest pet shop will show you the vast choice.

There is a distinct value in this merchandise. First, provided the food comes from a reputable manufacturer, it is certain to be wholesome and nutritious. The standard of inspection these days is high and, quite frankly, the fine aroma of some of these canned foods when opened has to be experienced to be believed. The fact that a dog owner can always have cans of dog food on hand has many advantages. It is good for the dog, for he gets a carefully balanced meal, and it suits the owner's convenience, for he can stock it without fear of deterioration and the routine of feeding is made simple and inexpensive. Canned food is usually three-quarters water; dry food is far the better buy.

Water

Water is important. It should be available at all times. In the house or kennels it should be changed at least twice a day, more frequently in hot weather. Remember that more than half the weight of the dog is composed of water, so a lot of water is required to maintain a chemical equilibrium. Of course if there is some medical reason why your dog should not have water, his allowance will have to be regulated. Some breeders collect rainwater for their dogs; they consider it more healthful than tap water, as it may well be.

Weight Control

It is unlikely that any member of a Beagle pack in regular use will put on excess weight for his work will keep him at an even level of hard muscle development. However, many pet dogs become obese and it is easy for a Beagle that is overfed and underexercised to put on fat. Fatness causes lassitude and often brings on ill health so care must be taken to make sure that your Beagle is kept well toned in muscle, and in generally firm condition. If you follow the directions already given for feeding and exercise this can be achieved quite easily.

A show dog will normally carry more weight than a hunt hound, size for size. The weight of the dog used for exhibition will have to be assessed by his owner to determine at what weight he looks best, for judges' opinions are personal and, of course, vary. At one show you might well be told your dog is too fat; at the next event a week later before a different judge he might be too spare, and yet the animal could be carrying exactly the same weight and distribution of weight.

Distribution of weight is important for keeping a dog's balance and appearance essential if he is to make his presence felt in the show ring. Some dogs, fortunately endowed physically, need little attention, but others need "shaping up" and it is with these that the skill of the owner can play an important part. This ability can only be applied by a person who knows what the ideal Beagle should look like, that is, one with an "eye for a dog" coupled with the know-how to put on the weight in the right spots. Here lies the reason for the success of some exhibitors, and in the reason for the failure of others, with identical Beagle material to work with. Therefore, take a close look at your dog. Does he seem to have to much spread in front? If he does, then this might be less apparent if he were leaner, and the same would apply if he is too short in back and a bit cloddy in appearance. Alternately, if he is too long in back or lacking depth, an extra few ounces may help disguise these deficiencies. A hound that is excessively overweight should never be exhibited. Much better to keep him at home and show him next time when you have removed some of the surplus. Quite apart from the abhorrence felt generally for a fat hound, the added avoirdupois will accentuate, in most cases, any faults he may already have.

The working Beagle does not usually present a weight problem. A hard running dog, especially one given his freedom, where he can chase rabbits to his heart's content, burns up a great deal of energy and will need all he can eat, especially of a high ration, to keep up his weight. In his case the distribution of weight is of no impor-

PURINA PET CARE CENTER

Weight control is as important to a Beagle as it is to a human. It is not usually a problem while young, but as an animal ages, his metabolism slows down and he requires fewer calories. The answer to the overweight adult house dog is simple: feed smaller meals!

tance. In the field, his ability, not his appearance, is what counts.

The answer to the overweight adult house dog is simple; feed smaller meals. Unfortunately, tenderhearted owners find it hard to resist the pleading in those soft brown eyes. It will help if they bear in mind that they are contributing to the possibility of their dog's suffering from a number of serious diseases and thereby shortening his life.

While your dog is still a puppy, teach him firmly that he is not to sit drooling alongside the table at mealtimes, and never, never drop tidbits from your plate. This discipline, well taught, will make it easier to control his diet in later years.

Nutrient Requirements

A great deal of work on dog nutrition is being done by governmental agencies. This work is not only investigatory but is also necessary because the government sets standards for pet food manufacturers. A summary of some of the findings of the Subcommitee on Canine Nutrition of the National Academy of Sciences condensed into chart form are given here.

Table I will be of interest to those who would like to prepare their own mix, and for those who are curious as to just what goes into a commercial dog food. It is a breakdown of two different meal-type rations.

Table I

Meal-Type Rations for Dogs [1]
(Dry matter 91%)

Ingredient	Ration 1 %	Ration 2 %
Meat and bone meal, 55% protein	8.00	15.00
Fish meal, 60% protein	5.00	3.00
Soybean oil meal	12.00	–
Soybean grits	–	19.00
Wheat germ oil meal	8.00	5.00
Skim milk, dried	4.00	2.50
Cereal grains	51.23	–
Corn flakes	–	26.75
Wheat bran	4.00	–
Wheat flakes	–	26.75
Fat, edible	2.00	–
Bone meal, steamed	2.00	–
Brewers yeast, dried	2.00	0.50
Fermentation solubles, dried	1.00	–
Salt, iodized	0.50	0.25
Vitamin A & D feeding oil (2,250 IU of A, 400 IU of D per gm)	0.25	0.50
Riboflavin supplement [2]	–	0.80
Iron oxide	0.02	–

[1] *While these rations have been used satisfactorily with some dogs, there is no assurance that all dogs will accept them readily.*

[2] *BY-500.*

It is unlikely that any member of the Beagle pack in regular use will put on excess weight, for his work will keep an even level of hard muscle development. American Champion Johnson's Fancy Beau, owned by Mr. Edward J. Johnson, is kept in perfect condition by regular exercise and careful diet control.

TOM CARAVAGLIA

Table II lists a dog's requirements in terms of food components per pound of body weight. It is interesting to note that growing puppies (last column) require two or more times as much of each of these nutrients as do adult dogs.

Table II

Nutrient Requirements of Dogs [1]
(Amounts per pound of body weight per day)

	Weight of dog in pounds	Adult maintenance	Growing puppies
Energy (kcal) [2]	5	50	100
	10	42	84
	15	35	70
	30	32	64
	50 and over	31	62
Protein-minimum (gm)		2.0	4.0
Carbohydrate-maximum (gm) [3]		4.6	7.2
Fat (gm)		0.6	1.2
Minerals:			
Calcium (mg)		120	240
Phosphorus (mg)		100	200
Iron (mg)		0.600	0.600
Copper (mg)		0.075	0.075
Cobalt (mg)		0.025	0.025
Sodium Chloride (mg)		170	240
Potassium (mg)		100	200
Magnesium (mg)		5	10
Manganese (mg)		0.050	0.100
Zinc (mg)		0.050	0.100
Iodine (mg)		0.015	0.030
Vitamins:			
Vitamin A (IU) [3]		45	90
Vitamin D (IU) [3]		3	9
Vitamin E (mg)		–	1
Vitamin B_{12} (mg)		0.0003	0.0006
Folic acid (mg)		0.002	0.004
Riboflavin (mg)		0.020	0.040
Pyridoxine (mg)		0.010	0.020
Pantothenic acid (mg)		0.023	0.045
Niacin (mg)		0.110	0.180
Choline (mg)		15	30

While the amount of food required by a dog varies, depending on such things as the dog's own metabolism, activity, environment, and so on, as we have previously noted, the greatest difference will be found between the requirements of a growing dog and an adult. Table III gives the estimated daily food intake required by dogs of various sizes, broken down into *Requirements for Maintenance* – this covers the average non-working dog under normal conditions – and *Requirements for Growth* – these are the amounts of food required by a growing dog While some adjustments in these amounts may be required for your own pet, they do serve as guidelines when estimating how much to feed your dog. An old dog will probably require less food than indicated here while a pregnant or nursing bitch will require more.

Table II Footnotes.

[1] *Symbols–gm = gram; mg = milligram; IU = International Unit.*

[2] *Values listed are for gross or calculated energy. Biologically available energy is ordinarily 75-85 per cent of the calculated.*

[3] [1] *The values shown are based upon dry and canned foods containing 91 and 28 per cent dry matter. Moisture has been included to indicate general level of composition rather than as a requirement. There is no evidence that carbohydrate as such is required, but since it occurs as a part of many dog food ingredients, a maximum value has been suggested.*

[2] *The 0.6 and 0.18 mg quantity of crystalline vitamin A is equal to 2000 and 600 IU, respectively. One mg vitamin A alcohol = 3,333 IU of vitamin A. One mg beta carotene = 1,667 IU of vitamin-A activity. For dogs carotene is approximately one-half as valuable as vitamin-A alcohol.*

[3] *These amounts of pure vitamin D correspond to 120 and 40 IU per pound of feed.*

Table III

Estimated daily food intakes required by dogs of various sizes.

	Requirements for maintenance			
	Dry type foods [1]		Canned dog food [2]	
Weight of dog	Per lb body wt	Per dog	Per lb body wt	Per dog
lbs	lbs	lbs	lbs	lbs
5	0.040	0.20	0.120	0.60
10	0.033	0.33	0.101	1.01
15	0.028	0.42	0.085	1.27
20	0.027	0.54	0.081	1.60
30	0.025	0.75	0.077	2.30
50	0.025	1.25	0.075	3.74
70	0.025	1.75	0.075	5.23
110	0.024	2.64	0.074	8.22

	Requirements for growth			
	Dry type foods [1]		Canned dog food [2]	
Weight of dog	Per lb body wt	Per dog	Per lb body wt	Per dog
lbs	lbs	lbs	lbs	lbs
5	0.080	0.40	0.240	1.20
10	0.066	0.66	0.202	2.02
15	0.056	0.84	0.190	2.54
20	0.054	1.08	0.160	3.20
30	0.050	1.50	0.154	4.60
50	0.050	2.60	0.150	7.48
70	0.050	3.50	0.150	10.46
110	0.048	5.28	–	–

For footnotes see page 97.

Treats made especially for dogs are fine between meals as rewards or to encourage playing, but they should not be fed to such an extent that they affect the dog's appetite.

Table III Footnotes

[1] *Dry foods contain 6-12 per cent moisture. Calculations of the amounts of dry food required have been based on energy supplied by food containing 91 per cent dry matter, 76 per cent protein plus carbohydrate, 5 per cent fat and 10 per cent ash, fiber and other inert material. This supplies a calculated 1583 kcal per pound, of which it is estimated that 80 per cent of 1266 kcal are digestible.*

[2] *Calculated on the basis of 28 per cent dry matter and the same nutrient ratios as in 1, which the total and available energy calculated as 490 and 415 (85 per cent of the total) kcal per pound.*

SALLY ANNE THOMPSON

A good stiff brush conscientiously applied will keep his coat in good order.

VIII Grooming

A short-coated breed, the Beagle, unlike some long-coated hounds, needs comparatively little attention paid to his toilet. The pack member should have his usual daily grooming, of course, as should every dog. A good stiff brush conscientiously applied will keep his coat in good order. Not only does brushing stimulate him and smarten his appearance, but it also gives his owner the opportunity of going over him regularly to check eye, ear and skin conditions. Anything untoward will be quickly noted by the experienced handler.

The show bench Beagle needs more exacting attention if he is to compete successfully for excellence of breed and appearance. First, he *must* be in good health and hard muscular trim. With such a foundation, your grooming work will be made easier. The well-groomed dog is always a credit to the groomer and himself.

Check initially to see that the coat is free from ticks and other parasites. It is better to remove these manually, that is with finger and thumb, or by dusting the dog with a good pesticide powder, than to trust to a bath to eliminate them.

Brushing

This is by far the more important grooming function. It should be done every day without fail. Much depends on the coat quality of your Beagle. Some dogs have coarse coats, others fine. Those with coarse coats need vigorous brushing, the others fare better with polishing and light treatment. How to brush is your prerogative, but the best kind of brush is the wire bristled type. Most of them are rubber seated. Such brushes are capable of getting through the coat, right down to the skin, without irritating it.

Whatever the quality of your Beagle's coat, parts of it will need special attention if you are to show your dog properly. The areas where the coat grows too long will have to be dealt with; these are usually on the lower reaches and the tip of the tail, the sides of the neck (or ruffs), the backs of the forelegs, thighs, and behind the ears. At these points, firm brushing is required to thin out the unwanted coat. Brush the shoulders and the rump to freshen the outline. Care must be taken not to brush with abandon, for the friction can irritate the skin.

Bathing

It is inadvisable to bathe a Beagle too often. Obviously, if he is dirty or has been soiled by some noxious substance during his travels, the necessity will arise. However, too many baths remove the natural oils from the coat and clog the pores which exude these secretions. A dog that is bathed too frequently can be detected by his indifferent coat. It will be dry and crisp, different from a staring coat. You will have to decide when to bathe him prior to a show, according to the texture of his coat. If he has a rather rough coat, accompanied by dry skin, three days before the show might be advisable. With a coat in good form, that is one with plenty of natural oils gracing it, 24 hours before the event will be in order.

The bath should be warm, never hot. Before you start it, make sure that the dog has had a chance to relieve himself, and that he has not recently been fed. In fact, it is best to bathe him at least two hours after a morning meal. Make sure that you have everything you are likely to need close at hand, especially if you are working alone, for dogs do not like baths, and if you must leave your Beagle to reach for something, he may well jump out of the

SALLY ANNE THOMPSON

Brushing is by far the most important grooming function. Pay particular attention to the areas where the coat grows too long; these are usually on the lower reaches and the tip of the tail, the sides of the neck, the backs of the forelegs, thighs, and behind the ears.

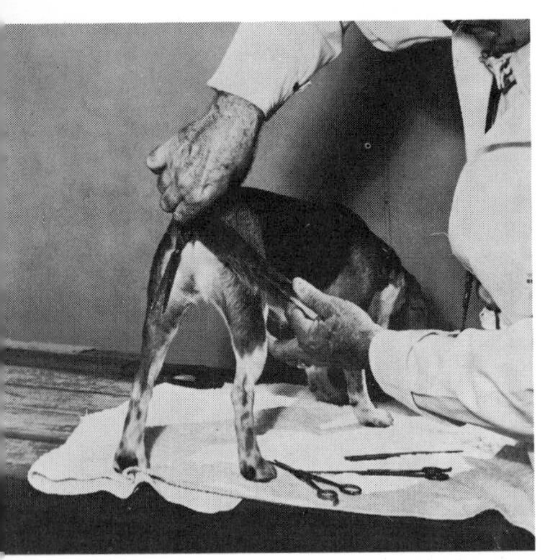

LOUISE VAN DER MEID

Ordinarily a Beagle does not require scissoring. However, in preparation for the show ring, areas where the coat grows too long will have to be dealt with. These include the backs of the thighs. These are not cut short, just the outline is tidied up.

LOUISE VAN DER MEID

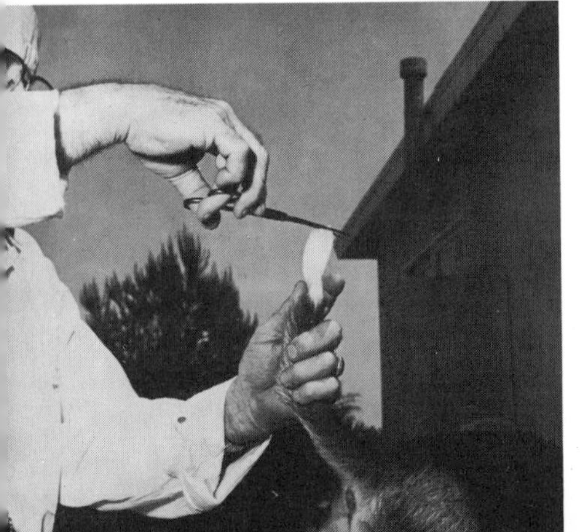

Check the tip of the tail preparatory to showing. If the hairs look scraggly, or if the outline is not nicely rounded, trim the excess length with scissors, being sure to maintain the natural appearance of the tip.

SALLY ANNE THOMPSON

The bath should be warm, never hot.

tub. It is a good idea to put a rubber mat on the bottom of the tub to prevent the dog's slipping and to have two good-sized Turkish towels handy – one to soak up the surplus moisture, the other to finish off with, especially around the eyes, ears, and genitals. A good-sized chamois leather is useful too. It is most effective in the final stage, after towelling, to get the coat good and dry.

There are a number of excellent dog soaps and shampoos on the market. Those with too much detergent or a high soda crystal content

LOUISE VAN DER MEID

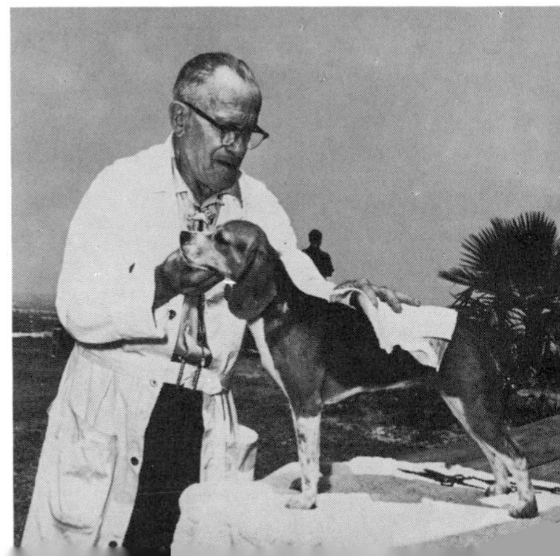

When bathing, a good-sized chamois skin is useful after toweling to get the coat good and dry.

SALLY ANNE THOMPSON

If you work where a bit of mess is of small consequence, let the Beagle shake himself. This will expel all the surface moisture and you can follow up with a towel and chamois until he is completely dry. Avoid outdoor bathing except under ideal conditions.

may be effective in removing dirt, but they work against coat quality. Have the shampoo ready and prepare two warm water rinses before you start. Work the shampoo well into the dog's coat, right down to his skin, so that when the rinse water is poured over him, all the dirt will be removed. Try and complete the job with one rinse so that when you pour over the second rinse it will act as added insurance against any remaining dirt.

If you work where a bit of mess is of small consequence, let the Beagle shake himself. This will dispel all the surplus moisture and you can follow up with the towel and chamois until he is completely dry. Keep him inside during the whole operation. Even under the best outdoor conditions, he is likely to catch a chill. Guard against the shampoo irritating his eyes by smearing the rims with some recommended eye ointment; the delicate inner ear can be protected with wads of cotton which have been smeared with a petroleum jelly like Vaseline.

It becomes incumbent upon you to make sure that the whole thing is done with as little fuss and discomfort as possible, otherwise, you may have difficulty in getting him to take a bath in the future. When you are certain that he is completely dry it is not so important to keep him in an even temperature. Make sure to remove his ear plugs and the protective grease from around his eyes. Check between his toes and thoroughly dry any dampness that remains.

Nails

The Beagle's toenails should be short. It is better to achieve this by regular exercise on pavements so that the nails are kept worn down to the ideal shortness; this will save clipping or filing. There are special dog nail clippers on the market which will do the job effectively; the guillotine type is the best. Care must be taken to insure that only the sharp tip is cut off. If too much is taken off the "quick" will bleed, often copiously. Should this occur, granulated sugar or powdered alum can be pressed into the wound.

It is better to keep the dog's toenails short by regular exercise so that the nails wear down naturally. There are special dog nailclippers on the market which will do the job effectively, should it become necessary.

SALLY ANNE THOMPSON

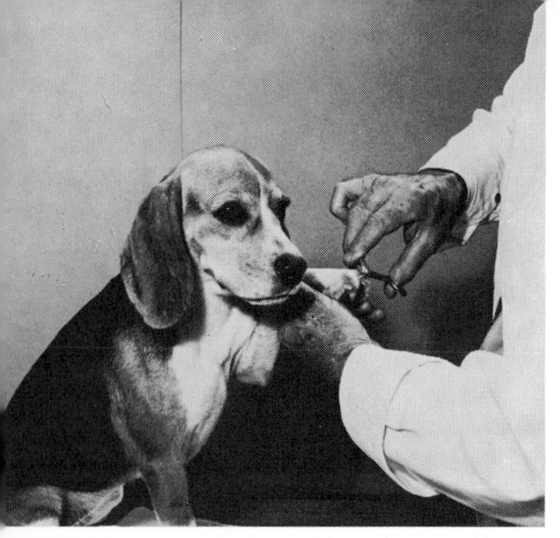
LOUISE VAN DER MEID

While the guillotine type of nailclipper is recommended for beginners, professionals frequently use the "nipper" type. Their use requires a little more care, but they are faster to work with.

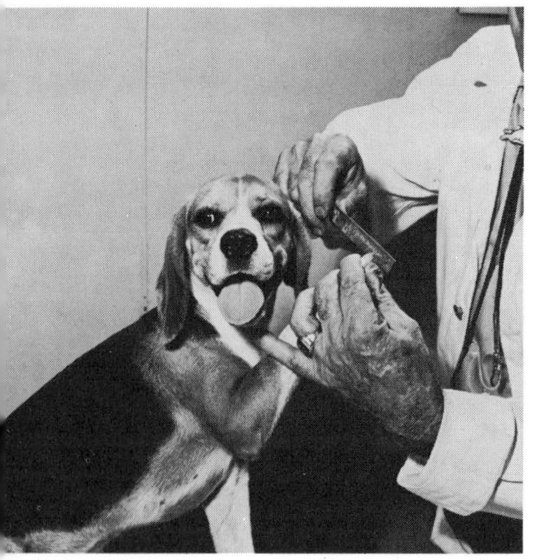
LOUISE VAN DER MEID

After clipping the nail to approximately the desired length, a coarse emery board or nail file may used to smooth and round the tip.

SALLY ANNE THOMPSON

A fine comb helps remove old hair to keep a coat healthy.

Foot Care

A Beagle worked irregularly often suffers from sore footpads. He will indicate his discomfort by constantly licking them. Frequently, the trouble is caused by interdigital cysts. Often, these can be remedied by a change of diet and this should be tried before surgery is considered.

However, some initial treatment is necessary. The foot should be soaked in *warm* water in which one tablespoonful of Epsom salts has been dissolved. The cyst will ripen with this treatment, and the pus within can be dispelled by gentle squeezing. The wound should then be lightly dusted with boric acid powder and inspected twice daily until it has healed.

It is important that no dampness be permitted to accumulate on the kennel floor, for dampness causes sore feet. The cause should be dealt with at once, and swabbing down always done before midday to allow the place to dry out. A Beagle's feet can be hardened by soaking them in an alum solution. This is made by dissolving four tablespoons of alum in one pint of lukewarm water. It will be found most effective.

Anal Glands

These are small glands situated on either side of the anus, an inheritance from the dog's wild ancestors. They were used originally to set his trail, but in these days the foul smelling fluid they exude may become congested and clog the glands, causing soreness and, in advanced cases, abscesses. The glands should receive treatment several times a year. The process is quite simple: take a pad of clean cotton, lift up the dog's tail with one hand and clamp the cotton pad across and under his anus with the other; then gently press inwards and slightly upwards with the finger and thumb. The obnoxious matter will be expelled onto the cotton which can then be burnt.

The Beagle usually indicates when this attention is imperative by turning around on himself as though being pricked in the rump, or by "tobogganing" along the ground on his hind end.

Eye Care

A dog's eyes usually indicate the condition of his health, good or bad. Eyes that are mattered-up, mucousy, or constantly watering

SALLY ANNE THOMPSON

Some people prefer to use a hound mitt in place of a brush, feeling that it makes it easier to control the dog and reach the less accessible areas.

are always suspect, so unless you are very sure no illness is impending it is well to invoke the assistance of your veterinarian. Simple forms of Conjunctivitis (inflamed or weeping eyes) can be dealt with at home. There are several reliable preparations available at your pet department to combat this condition. These, or sterilized cod liver oil, are effective if applied daily, and as their gentle action will ease most complaints an occasional drop or smear on the lower lid will be appreciated.

Troubles such as *Ectropion,* when the eyelids turn slightly outwards and fail to give protection from dust and pollen, and *Entropion,* a hereditary condition of the eyes, in which the eyelids turn inward and the lashes rub on the eyeballs, are both extremely painful complaints, but fortunately, not common in Beagles. Both must be dealt with by a qualified veterinarian. *Entropion* requires surgery.

SALLY ANNE THOMPSON

Clean your dog's ears regularly, particularly the flaps. Do not reach or poke down further than you can see.

Ear Care

Beagles can suffer from a number of ear conditions, although daily attention to the ears will greatly overcome them. The initial symptoms are constant scratching, some head shaking, and evidence of acute discomfort. As dogs have no fingers to poke their ears when they're uncomfortable, they must scratch them. The commonest form of ear complaint which beset the Beagle is *Canker*, of which two types exist. One affects the edges of the ears and the lobes, the other the ear canal. The external form can be caused by cuts or grazes which have become infected. These can be dealt with simply by bathing them with an antiseptic after they have been washed clean; then apply boric acid powder.

The internal type of canker is not so easy to cure. The lining of the ear will be found inflamed and warm to the touch. The dog

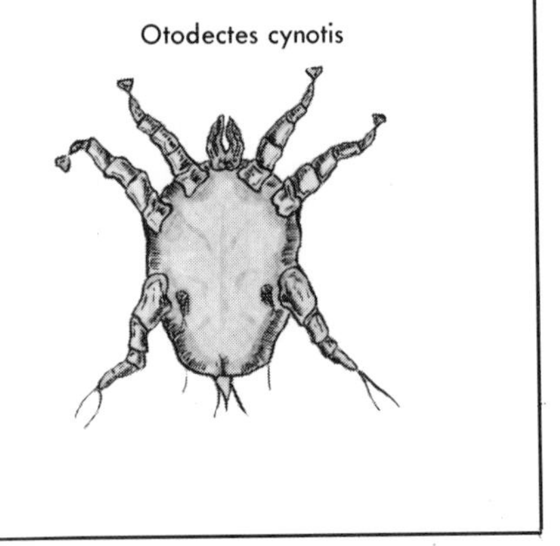

CHET PLEGGE, D.V.M

Otodectes cynotis. The presence of the ear mite may be indicated by a dry, crumbly brown substance in the dog's ear. The mite may be seen under a low power microscope (100x). This condition should never be neglected.

LOUISE VAN DER MEID

A Beagle does not require clipping, but the whiskers are trimmed in preparation for a show.

LOUISE VAN DER MEID

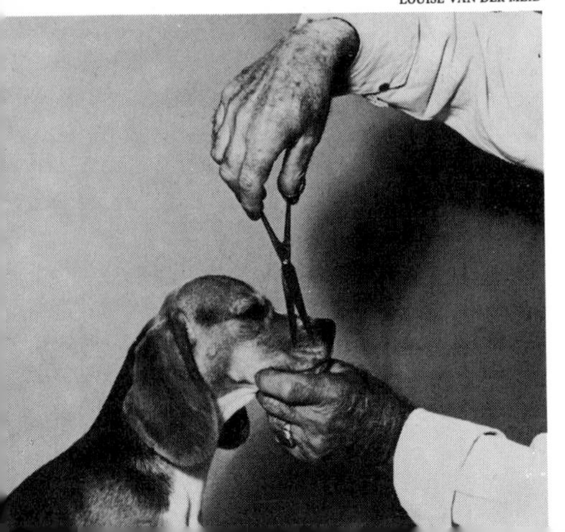

Whiskers and eyebrows may be trimmed to improve the outline of the show Beagle. However, this is a touchy job. Use blunt-tipped scissors, and always point them away from the dog's face, particularly the eyes and ears, so that if he moves suddenly he won't be injured.

will be in considerable discomfort, scratching the ear, often drawing blood. The channel of the ear will be filled with a waxy, sticky brown substance which often has an unpleasant odor. If the wax is dry and crumbly, it may indicate ear mites which require specific treatment to eradicate them. Care should be taken when handling the ear for it is a delicate organ; rough or haphazard treatment can cause permanent damage. There are several excellent commercial lotions on the market for dealing with canker and one should be used after cleaning the ear. Some of the waxy substance can be removed with finger and thumb; other particles lower down can be gently teased out, first by manipulating the ear to loosen them, then by extracting them with the aid of sterilized tweezers or cotton-tipped swabs. The healing process can be hastened by inserting a half teaspoonful of boric acid powder into the ear twice a day.

If the patient still seems distressed and unable to sleep well, one tranquilizing tablet may be given before he retires. If he persists in scratching it may be necessary to employ an Elizabethan collar: two half-circles of cardboard fitted around the neck.

During every grooming session inspect your Beagle's ears carefully since, to repeat, this is one of the breed's most vulnerable points, and unless you are an experienced breeder it is probably wiser to consult a veterinarian for any ear troubles that do not clear up within a day or so.

The routine cleaning of the Beagle's ears is simple. Never use soap and water. Clean them with a cotton swab dipped in peroxide, alcohol or olive oil. Never probe deeper than you can see. There are several good medicated earwashes on the market. Ask your pet shop owner to recommend one.

Care of the Teeth

The Beagle's teeth should be checked regularly. Food particles lodged there can be just as damaging as when lodged in yours. Dogs who are allowed to gnaw on big bones, hardbaked dog biscuits, hard rubber or rawhide toys generally manage to keep their teeth in good condition. Tartar can be kept from forming by regular brushing. Use a man's hard bristle toothbrush and a mixture of pumice, salt and baking soda. If a toothbrush bothers the dog, use a rough washcloth instead. Since too great an accumulation of tartar can loosen a dog's teeth, have a veterinarian scale it off.

SALLY ANNE THOMPSON

The training collar is frequently miscalled a choke chain. The purpose of using this type of collar is not to choke, but to train. Except when the dog is pulling vigorously, it will hang loosely about his neck. To use it properly, hold the handle of the lead in your right hand, take the slack in your left; when the dog pulls, jerk the lead sharply, relax it immediately, and say "No!" or "Heel!", or whatever command is appropriate to the occasion.

IX Training and Handling

A good deal of patience is needed by the dog trainer who wants to succeed. It is not always easy to maintain one's self control at the end of a long session with an awkard pupil, but it is an important lesson which must be learned before commencing to train a dog. Many promising young dogs have been ruined because their trainers lacked patience. Even a dog considered almost fully trained can be spoiled by one outburst of the trainer's temper. The experienced handler knows that no matter how well a dog behaves, no matter how well he appears to have been trained, there will come a time when he will show resistance or indifference. Disregard such a lapse for it may be that the dog has gone stale, and it is better to allow him a little relaxation.

The trainer always should keep a calm mind, a gentle voice, a soft hand, and a ready understanding of his pupil. With all these things he is well charged to perform his task and can achieve good results.

Persistence is another necessary attribute, for repetition is the way of sinking a requirement into a dog's intellect. In effect, the trainer will have to give the dog the same lesson day in and day out until the animal fully understands what is wanted of him, and can do it without thinking, for after a while dogs come to perform their lessons reflexively. There should always be some rewarding tidbits near at hand, but the dog should not be given one unless he has deserved it.

Errors should always be corrected gently but firmly, and with no show of temper. A lot depends on the individual you are handling. Clearly a gentle dog must not be handled the same way as a "varminty" specimen. Each pupil's temperament, particularly, needs understanding. No dog is the same as his neighbor and he must be respected as an individual and treated as one.

Initial training must be slow and careful for you will be learning about your charge as you go along. You will find idiosyncrasies that can be used to good effect in training. Keep an eye open for them, especially when teaching tricks. Very often, a dog by his own mannerisms or canine humor, is already halfway to performing a trick. It is up to the trainer to reinforce and perfect it.

Most dogs respond to training. Any Beagle of average intelligence will make a ready pupil. Occasionally, one is unfortunate enough to get a stupid creature who will not, or does not want to, respond to lessons. Even these can be improved with persistence, but not after it is finally realized that the time being spent could more profitably be applied to training a more responsive dog.

The important thing to remember when training your Beagle is that you must gain his confidence. Once he trusts you and feels secure in your presence you will have surmounted the biggest obstacle and the rest will be comparatively easy sailing. His training should commence the moment he becomes yours. The business of making him house-broken and leash-trained has already been discussed; matters like Field and Obedience training as well as Show Ring education should be attempted only after these elementary lessons have been mastered.

Elementary Field Training

The finest way for a Beagle puppy to learn manners in the field is to take him (with others, if possible) on the hunt. This teaches him how to behave with stock, makes him wise about cover, and encourages him to become adjusted to the scents and ways of the denizens of the woods. He will quickly discover what a fine nose he has and employ it naturally because of his wonderful Beagle heritage.

With functional breeds such as the Beagle, it is better to allow them the opportunity of self-expression in their work rather than to attempt some individual form of tutelage. A well-bred Beagle has it in him to trail game, and the degree of skill with which he does it determines whether he is a first-class or mediocre hound. He will have to master the commonly used words of command, for to be of use to his owner he must be tractable. It is usual to walk the puppy with the hunt when he is around two months of age just to get him acclimatized, but it is unwise to introduce him to the field proper until he is at least four months old. Many masters favor pups that are several months older than this since some youngsters are very slow starters. Much depends on the Beagle himself – a boisterous, disorderly type of puppy had better be left until he has settled down, even if it means waiting until he is a year old; another youngster with a stable, equable disposition can begin work early in life.

Some owners start their Beagles off on tame rabbits. Although this may be effective, it is not as good as giving a youngster the sight of a wild one for his first lesson. The Beagle will soon learn to depend on his nose rather than this eyes and, although his first sight of game will send him chasing after it pell-mell, once he has taken in its fresh smell it will be this which guides him to the quarry scent, and, more than any other factor, awaken his natural tendencies.

It should never be forgotten that the young Beagle must be trained to be steady when loose. This applies not only to the field dog but to the pet Beagle. If he chases cattle and poultry he can prove a nuisance, if not a liability. This habit demands severe punishment on the first misdemeanor but to be effective you must catch him in the act; to emphasize the punishment take him back to the scene of his crime on a long rope and repeat the punishment if he persists in chasing the wrong quarry. If he is an intelligent dog, he will not repeat his first false step. If he does, as soon as he starts toward the cattle or poultry, drag him back vigorously for another lesson. This will soon steady even the most recalcitrant Beagle.

Obedience Training

The following training exercises are the most important. The pet dog owner should consider them too, for they will bring about a happy relationship between dog and master. The dog enjoys life more, for by obeying he knows he is pleasing his master, and the master, by showing interest in his pet and finding him tractable gets more pleasure from the dog. The best age to begin serious training is about nine months, but some preparations can be started before then.

Come

The first lesson in obedience that the young dog should learn is to *come when called.* Nothing is more irksome than the dog that refuses to come at the word of command. If you have ever tried to catch an elusive puppy, one that ignores your exhortations and treats the chase as one big game, you will understand! You should never chase the youngster – the more you do this, the more you will have to keep it up, increasing your frustration. The Golden Rule is to be calm. Have a tasty tidbit in your hand and call the puppy gently by name, and give the command "Come!" Eventually, he will oblige. Give him the tidbit and a pat on the head along with a few words of praise.

After a few lessons he will know that something pleasant awaits him when he comes to you. Try and avoid putting him on lead every time you are successful in retrieving him. He will associate this with an end to his freedom and not like the idea. To get the best results teach this exercise when the pupil is hungry. If he seems difficult, it may be necessary to use a light check cord to make him come, but do this only to prevent his doing what *he* wants to do. Never use the cord to pull him towards you; rather use it to correct his movements. Use your voice, cajolery, and tidbits just as if no cord were there.

Sit

The command to "Sit" is next in importance. The dog should be so trained that every time you halt, he sits immediately at your left heel. This is a highly practical exercise. Your dog should be moving on a loose lead close to you; a position you will encourage by having a tidbit in your left hand, close to his nose. Stop suddenly and at the same time give the command "Sit!" As you do so swing your body around to the left without moving your feet, holding your right hand over the dog's head. The average pupil will look up at your right hand and if you synchronize your hand action with the halt and your word of command, he will go down on his rear at once. The secret lies in the unison of word and action.

However, there will be some dogs who do not conform. Such a dog will have to be forced into the sitting position by taking his collar in your right hand, pulling him back, and pushing him down on his rump with your left hand. If you find that when he sits he sits too far from you, do not move towards him or drag him to you; move away from him and encourage him towards your left leg with your left hand.

Down

The next command is the "Down". It is quite a simple procedure. The lead, from the dog's collar to your hand should pass under your left foot. To get the dog down, pull up the lead with the right hand at the same time you push down the dog with your left. At the same time say "Down!" in an authoritative tone. Most dogs have a natural tendency to cringe when shouted at, and the trainer should take full advantage of this. In effect, the loud command will get him part of the way down, the least tension and the pushing down will complete the exercise. The cringing, which you are using to your own advantage, will disappear once the dog learns what you want of him. Some trainers prefer to break this into two commands, giving "Sit" first and then "Down."

Stay

Along with the exercises "Sit" or "Down", it is advisable to train your dog to "Stay". Many pupils who learn to "Sit" and "Down" readily find it difficult to stay in one position for any length of time. The most comfortable position for your dog is the "Down". When he is comfortably downed, stand in front of him, giving the command "Stay" and move back one step. If he starts to move, get him into the "Down" position again and repeat "Stay!" Eventually he will catch on, and you can begin to lengthen the distance between you by gradually moving back until there is considerable space. This has to be done by degrees, of course, to give the dog confidence. But before long you will be able to go completely out of his sight and remain there for extended intervals.

Heeling

Training to heel was mentioned earlier, for it really is one of the first exercises that should be taught. It is a good foundation for all later exercises, since it conditions the dog to accept training.

Stand with the dog on your left side, both facing the same way. The lead should be in your right hand and it should be long enough, and held in such a way, that the slack of its loop hangs halfway between the dog's neck and the ground. Calling the dog by name, move forward with the command "Heel!" As you are likely to precede the dog, jerk him forward with the right hand, and pat him with the left hand; reward him with a tidbit and words of praise. This exercise repeated enough times will get good results. It can be followed by unleashing the dog and repeating the same routine with him loose. This is known as the "heel free" exercise and it will show how well he has learned his lesson on lead. If his work is poor, put him back on the leash and resume his "on-leash" training.

Remember that the dog should always be on your left side. Your right hand should be the one holding the lead; in effect, the correcting hand, whereas the left hand is always the rewarding and caressing, as well as the guiding, one. The importance of giving a dog a lot of petting as a reward for good work cannot be too strongly stressed. You should not be lax in your encouragement, nor should you allow a command to go unheeded or disobeyed. Dogs

SALLY ANNE THOMPSON

"Heel!" Hold the handle of the leash in your right hand, take the slack in your left, call the dog by name and move forward with the command "Heel!"

are quick to take advantage if advantage is given, and any concession you make or fault you condone will only retard progress.

The object in "Heel" is to train the dog to maintain a position just to your left with his head parallel to and alongside your left leg. As you move he moves also; as you turn he turns with you, and when you stop he smartly assumes a sitting position by your side, for all the world like a shadow attached by invisible bonds. For optimum results his attention must be riveted upon his master and he should allow nothing to distract his attention.

Show Training

In training a dog for show bench work, it is necessary to concentrate on three main lessons, which are:

1. To stand still, naturally and firmly, while the judge is looking at him.
2. To tolerate, without moving, the judge's examination of his structural conformation his mouth, eyes, ears, tail, and private parts.
3. To move freely and in typical Beagle fashion up and down the length of the show ring on a slack lead, confidently and with his head up.

Some hounds, having a penchant for ringcraft, save the trainer many hours of work and patience. An exhibitor with such a dog is fortunate indeed! However, almost all dogs can be trained and if you have a potential winner, the hours you are going to spend on his show ring training will be profitable.

Early training can be started when the puppy is about five months old. He should have had some elementary obedience and lead training before this, of course, as it will stand him in good stead for he will have learned to please you and enjoy doing what he has been told. Along with this, it would be a good idea to get him used to a bit of mild pummeling such as a judge might administer in going over with him. With this, the family might be prevailed upon to help, along with an occasional visitor. Get them to open his mouth, look at his teeth, run their hands over his ears, down his neck, round his ribs, lift up his forelegs to examine his bone texture and generally prod him about. He will wonder what it is all about, but being a Beagle he will be keen to learn. If he is hungry, the

TOM CARAVAGLIA

A show dog like American Champion Johnson's Fancy Beauty must learn to stand still, naturally and firmly, while the judge is looking at him.

tidbits you give him for learning well will please him and bring good results. He should always be on his lead because you will need to control him.

Try him out first and see if he stands naturally without assistance. Some dogs do, and usually the natural stance is preferable to one that has been taught by manual placing. A sound, well-constructed dog of good type should need no help in this department, but it often becomes necessary to place a puppy in the desired show position. It wil be found that after a number of successful lessons he will automatically fall into the position he has been trained to, so make sure that your placing is the correct one. Do not spread his front legs out too much or his hind legs too far under him. Place one hand under his chest between the forelegs, the other hand under his rear; lift him slightly and set him down truly and firmly.

The front legs should drop down in a straight line from shoulders to the ground when viewed from the front, and from the elbows to the ground when seen from the side. The back feet should run parallel with the front feet; in fact, the dog should stand in a rectangle when viewed from above. When he is rightly placed, the command "Stand" should be given and repeated every time he is so placed.

At first, he will be confused, but with the incentive of reward tidbits and a deal of caressing for his progress, better than average results can be expected. Remember that the training of a puppy should never last for more than ten or fifteen minutes at any one time.

When he has shown progress as a solo exhibit, it is time to introduce some distractions, for he will have plenty of these when he is shown. Arrange for a few other owners with their dogs to walk around him. Train him in a more public place so that strangers are brought into the picture; all of these things will help him when he finally enters the show ring. He should be moved up and down an imaginary ring. Show rings vary little in their dimensions so you can approximate the distance he must get used to. Move around and back and forth with him, as if you were exhibiting him to a judge.

Pace

The Beagle should be paced at a speed that suits him if he is to give good effect in movement. A correctly formed specimen will move properly; bad movement usually comes from structural deficiencies. If your dog, when going away from you, moves with his hind legs parallel with no sign of cow-hocks or in-toes, and, when coming to you, his forelegs are parallel and do not "paddle", you have very good material with which to work. The speed at which he moves, already mentioned, is important.

A good dog, capable of taking the judge's eye, can lose out completely if his type, style and conformation are detracted from by taking him away too fast or bringing him forward too slowly. The dog needs to move with his head up and on a slack lead, his body almost level with your own as you progress up and down the show ring. If the lead is slack, your Beagle will probably fall into his natural gait; this will be the correct one, the one to show off his points best. However, if he is moving ahead of you on a taut lead, his action will be wrong for his head will thrust forward and his shoulders be thrown out. If he is dragging back, his hindquarters will not be showing all the thrust and smooth power of which they are capable. Even when moving freely on a slack lead, a hazard exists; the dog, not being fully trained to accept distractions, will be affected in the manner of his gait by the bustle and atmosphere of the ring. He may move too much like a trotting pony, or be choppy in his action.

You should be *aware* of your dog at all times. When he shows some undesirable trait you must eradicate it immediately; herein lies the vital importance of knowing your breed, for without understanding, you will find it impossible to recognize faults. However, the patient application (along with enthusiasm) and with daily practice your dog will soon be ready for his first show.

A Few Tricks

A lot of people like to teach their dogs to perform. Some very amusing parlor tricks can be taught to any dog of average intelligence, but before training your dog to do a few, it is best to make sure that you are not going to teach him any trick which he is likely to do when being judged in the show ring! That is, of course, if you propose to exhibit him. For example, the popular "Shake Hands" trick is somewhat risky if you intend to show your dog. He is quite likely to sit down in the middle of the ring and shake hands with the judge! It might make him the center of attraction and get a big laugh, but it will not help him win a prize.

However, if you fancy seeing your dog perform a trick or two, try the simple ones first. The popular "Shake Hands" is simple enough. Get your dog into a sitting position, and give the command "Shake Hands" or maybe "Paw", taking hold of his right paw gently, lifting it and shaking it, then returning it. Give him a reward tidbit and repeat the exercise several times. He will soon get the idea.

Another trick is to teach him to beg. Again, get him into a sitting position. Take hold of both paws this time and lift them up until

SALLY ANNE THOMPSON

Some dogs will pose for showing naturally, without assistance. Usually the natural stance is preferable to one that has been taught by manual placing.

he is in the approved begging position. Make sure he is properly balanced, then release his paws so that he remains up, finding his own balance for a few moments. Give him a reward for maintaining this position, which you can improve by holding the tidbit right over his nose, repeating the command 'Beg" all the time. Soon he will remain in the position for long periods, but remember he should always be rewarded when he does well.

You can enlarge on the "Beg" trick, once he has mastered it, by balancing a biscuit or dog treat on his nose as he begs. He should be warned not to take the tidbit until you say so. At first, he will try to shake off the treat, but put it back or keep it on the top of his nose with the cup of your palm. Take your hand away

SALLY ANNE THOMPSON

and he will stand begging with the treat balanced on his nose waiting for you to say "Take it!" At this, some dogs get very dextrous, and on command will toss the treat into the air and catch it on the way down or twist their muzzles sideways and let it slide into their mouths.

Most dogs enjoy doing tricks, but it is not fair to insist on teaching too many at once.

The Beagle as a Watchdog

Beagles are essentially good-natured dogs. They are cheerful and they love people. Nevertheless, they do have a keen nose, a sharp sense of hearing, and they are always on the alert. These are characteristics which give them the ability to become excellent home guardians, and with a little training they prove excellent at the job. However, it is difficult to make an attack dog out of a Beagle. He is just too cheerful, believing that all the world is his friend.

In spite of this, if you make a sport or a game out of his being a watchdog he will respond eagerly and soon prove himself a master at the job. Actually, he should really be called an alarm dog rather than a guard dog. He doesn't attack, but with his great big hound voice he will certainly let the neighborhood know when there is a prowler about.

As I said, make a game of it. When someone knocks at the door react excitedly. Slap the table or your tigh, clap your hands, turn to your Beagle with a high pitched tone of voice and say, "Who's there? Who's there? What is it?" Your excitement will communicate itself to the dog and chances are that he'll get up and come to you to see what is going on. When he does, run to the door, slap on it, again clap your hands and again by your manner and voice attempt to get him to bark.

When he does, pet him and let him know that this is what you expect of him. After a few lusty barks say, "That's a good boy! Quiet! Quiet!" and hold his mouth closed. When he subsides, reward him.

"Beg!" is an appealing trick, and one easily taught to a mature dog. Give the reward for maintaining this position, which you can improve by holding the tidbit right over his nose.

SALLY ANNE THOMPSON

Normally, Beagles are not used as retrievers, but there is no reason why your pet cannot learn to fetch a ball. In addition to being a lot of fun, it's good exercise. Hold it in front of his nose and tease him with it until he shows an interest; then if he tries to take it, toss it a few inches away and give the command "Fetch!" The distance can gradually be extended.

Repeat this performance as often as necessary, and, if necessary, with the aid of an accomplice, until he gets the idea that when someone comes to the door or makes any noise outside the house he must bark in order to receive a reward. He must also learn that when you say QUIET!, he is to stop barking. Eventually, of course, the reward can be dispensed with.

TOM CARAVAGLIA

Lady B of Lincoln Field with Johnson's Fancy Black Joe. Lady B (smaller) is half field-bred and half show-bred, resulting in a smaller, lighter dog. Johnson's Fancy Black Joe is a show type stud dog. When mated with another show dog, his puppies will be large and blocky like himself.

X Heredity in the Beagle

Every conscientious Beagle breeder will want to improve the breed. He can become an important cog in the machinery of this evolution by either allowing his fine male to be used at stud only to worthy bitches, or by breeding his own bitch in such a way that her off-

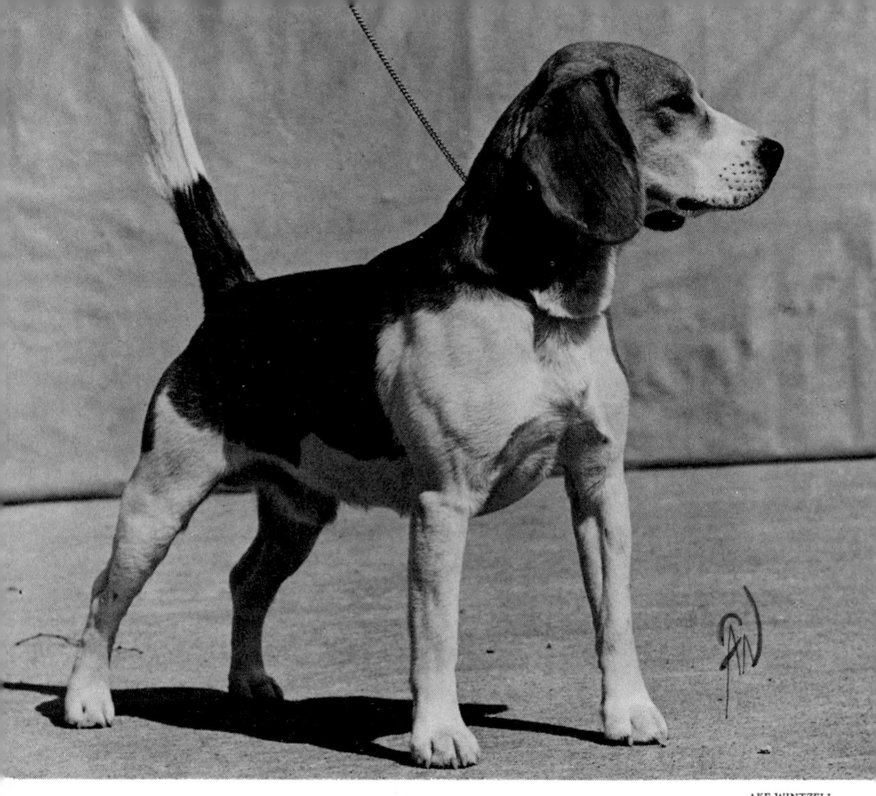

AKE WINTZELL

The Beagle is a remarkably uniform dog. Here we see a Swedish Champion looking like an English or American show type. Perhaps he is a little leggier, but still well within the Standard.

spring will be improvements on herself. Admittedly, this needs planning and not a small measure of skill, although it is on record that many a one bitch owner, breeding her for her health's sake only, has found a champion or two in the litter! Such occasions are, of course, rare, but there is no valid reason why even a novice should not aim to bring first-class Beagles into the world, dogs better than their parents.

The average breeder's knowledge of genetics is scant, and not everyone can assimilate with ease such scientific data, but there is no excuse for not knowing the Beagle Standard, and it is of vital importance to know it well before embarking on any breeding project. In the breeder's mind there should be a constant picture of the ideal specimen. This perfect Beagle becomes the target at which to aim when selecting the mate for your dog or bitch.

Inbreeding

This is planned breeding, mating closely related dogs, in both of whom exist to a marked degree certain wanted characteristics, in order to establish these points firmly in the offspring. As a general practice, inbreeding is hazardous and should be utilized only by experienced breeders, for while it can fix desirable features, it can, at the same time, perpetuate the bad ones that have been lying latent (recessives) somewhere back along the bloodline of the related parents. Such inbreeding can bring out hidden mental and physical deficiencies, including epilepsy, blindness, cryptorchidism, monorchidism and sterility, so it is important that breeders planning to employ inbreeding should know what they are doing. Inbreeding includes the following crosses:

Mother to Son
Father to Daughter
Brother to Sister

Linebreeding

Although similar to inbreeding in that related dogs are mated, linebreeding takes considerably longer to establish purity of strain because the degree of the relationship of the dogs used is not as close. Unlike inbreeding, which involves culling the unwanted specimens produced by its more drastic methods, linebreeding is a considerably less radical process that aims at the same thing, but achieves its results over the longer term in a safer way. To linebreed, the breeder aims for the characteristics he wants, either directly or indirectly, by arranging matings with the descendants of the good dog which has attracted him. Only specimens of high physical and temperamental worth should be used, and if certain points are desired, the parent union should be between dogs with a full measure of these wanted points, although, possibly, one may have them only in moderation. Linebreeding includes the following crosses:

Grandsire to Granddaughter
Granddam to Grandson
Aunt to Nephew
Uncle to Niece

AKE WINTZELL

The desire to perpetuate the blood lines of a winning dog has resulted in a considerable amount of inbreeding and linebreeding.

Technically speaking, linebreeding would also include those closer matings which are sometimes considered inbreeding, such as:

Half-sister to Brother

First Cousin to Cousin

Some breeders call it linebreeding when a common ancestor appears twice within the last five generations. This, however, extends the term too far, as it is common to find this happening even when linebreeding has not been intended. As with all forms of calculated breeding, it is of vital importance to make sure that the parents do at least conform to a desired type, and that they are healthy and sound in all respects. Care must be taken to make sure that no undesirable feature, possibly one unsuspected from previous ancestry, is allowed to rise. Such characteristics are capable of causing reversion to an early and usually unwanted type. Once roused, unwanted traits are often difficult to eradicate and the line, instead of receiving the improvement planned for it, is rendered a grave disservice.

Out-Breeding

This is sometimes, less correctly, termed outcrossing. It refers to the mating of a pair that have no common relationship in their ancestry. The general idea is to produce some desired characteristics which such a union *may* achieve. However, it is a rather "hit-or-miss" process and unwanted attributes, hitherto unknown in the line can easily arise. In this form of breeding, although ancestry will show no common denominator, it is important to match type at least. The resultant litter may well prove not uniform in size and with no wanted characteristic showing in any of its members, although they, in their productive cycle, may produce puppies which evince the points desired. In the case of field trial dogs, less importance is given to appearance and more to rabbit running ability.

Frequently an outcross is arranged to dilute undesirable traits or to introduce desirable ones into a strain. The most desirable of the litter is then bred back to the parent and a system of line or in-breeding initiated.

Initial Application

As has already been emphasized, it is important to know what a good Beagle looks like, and how one acts in the field, before trying to produce good ones! The beginner's first lesson having been to understand and interpret the Standard of the breed, his next endeavor should be to apply his knowledge to the living Beagle. The best place to do this is at the specialist shows where only Beagles are exhibited, or field trials where Beagles compete. Here will be seen many of the best Beagles, quite a number of mediocre ones, and a few very poor specimens. Almost any exhibit or field trial handler will be pleased to display his Beagle to an admirer, and from indifferent specimens, as well as from superb examples, much can be learned.

The early stages of this self-education should be spent at dog shows, watching the judging. Sit at the ringside and watch the Beagles enter the ring, view them as they line up to be judged and

AKE WINTZELL

It is important to know what a good Beagle looks like, and how one acts in the field, before trying to produce good ones. You are much more likely to obtain satisfactory results by breeding from the best, rather than from mediocre specimens.

are moved up and down the ring by the handler for assessment of their movement and soundness. Form your own personal conclusions as to which should be the winner: the second, third, and so on. Make notes against the names of the exhibits in your catalog. If its margins are not wide enough, have a notebook with you. Enter such things as, "seems too big"; "feet too close together in front"; "front too narrow"; "badly behaved"; "poor coat", and similar straightforward comments without attempting technicalities.

Discuss the various points with other owners present. If you talk to the right ones, and the right ones are usually those who have achieved the most success, you will learn a lot. Most Beagle people are friendly and ready to help the novice. Nevertheless, success is seldom achieved without a deal of hard work, and you cannot expect a successful breeder to allow his brains to be picked bare. Temper your inquiries, and be thankful for a few pearls of wisdom for many of the things you learn will help you to avoid the pitfalls that would ordinarily lie in your path.

At a field trial you will not be able to watch the whole show because the gallery does not follow the dogs; only the owners and judges are close enough to watch every twist and turn, retrieves or losses, and all the exquisite differences in the dogs' actions by which winners are chosen. However, you will see some of the action and hear the comments after each heat. You can base your judgment of the many dogs' capabilities on these.

Remember, though, that not every chance remark you hear carries weight. At shows and trials you will find a fair sprinkling of jealous handlers, for dog exhibition – have no doubt about it – is often a fiercely competitive pastime. From such fault finders you may overhear spiteful, often untrue comment, and it will behoove you to separate fact from fiction.

Planned Parenthood

Today, the breeding of dogs is a science. The subject requires a considerable amount of time in study as well as in careful programming. Of course, good Beagles have been known to turn up from chance hit-or-miss matings, as we have already said. However, these mutations (as they are known in scientific circles) or "sports" are seldom of true worth, apart from their personal appearance, for when they are required to procreate their own strong points, they are usually dismal failures. And yet it is by perpetuating these mutations, when they are of value, that improvement is made.

A successful breeder needs to know the genetic background not only of his bitch, but of the stud dog he intends to use. This means that he should have in mind a clear picture of:

a The physical appearance and temperament of each and every dog and bitch in the ancestry of the parents, as far back as three generations at least. If he is fortunate enough to have had length of time in the breed, or a reliable reference which

(Overleaf) This is a fine looking, pet type Beagle. The chances of a dog like this having show quality puppies are negligible. If you want to breed winners, you must breed from winners. CREDIT: SALLY ANNE THOMPSON

will allow him to be acquainted with animals even further back, so much the better.

b The knowledge of the good and faulty points of all these animals, correctly assessed in relation to the requirements of the breed Standard, which he should fully understand. Further, it is desirable that he know the transmittal of possibilities of these points, the degree of chance involved in their being passed on to the progeny.

He will find that certain dog families have fixed features of type, style and temperament. One strain might excel in head properties, another fail in hindquarters, yet another lack expression, although show marked style of gait.

From the best of the various families he will want to draw "parts" to build up his perfect strain. It is rather like building your own automobile – taking the outstanding components from a number of motor cars, and putting them together so that the finished vehicle appears to be a near faultless machine. Like building an auto, it is far from an easy task, for while the components selected might stand alone, intrinsically and functionally perfect, together they fall far short of the ideal.

It is an interesting facet of dog breeding that you might produce the perfect head, the perfect ears, the perfect expression, the perfect body, legs and feet, the perfect quarters, tail and type, and yet when all are joined together in the whole dog, the result is nothingness. One possible reason could be poor movement due to unsoundness, but the usual reason is that the good points do not *flow* into the whole to make a perfect picture. Experimentation will eventually take care of such problems, of course, but the process is wearying and time consuming. Setbacks are inevitable when attempting to breed good dogs, but every setback should be analyzed carefully so that something is learned from it.

Physiology of Reproduction

Every conscientious breeder should understand the biological process which produces his dogs. It is an involved subject and no attempt will be made to cover it in this book, apart from this brief look.

Twice a year, usually, the bitch's ovaries develop follicles. Each

SALLY ANNE THOMPSON

Breeding a dog is something like building your own automobile: you take the outstanding components from a number of specimens and through breeding try to put them together, so the finished animal is nearly faultless. You might start with a dog like Lee's Visit shown here which has an outstanding head.

follicle contains an ovum or egg, which progresses gradually to the surface of the ovary, and, in due course, breaks through into the sac surrounding the ovary; this occurs at perhaps the fifteenth day of the bitch's heat. If she has been mated with a dog, some of his semen is waiting in the sac; the sperm at once attacks the eggs and each egg is penetrated by a sperm. The eggs are thus fertilized.

Genes

The egg has within its nucleus many tiny "packets" of chemicals called genes. Except for the genes controlling sex, these are paired. A gene is thought to control the facets of heredity, and the interaction between genes determines the traits of the individual being formed. The egg contains twice as many genes as the sperm, which possesses only one of each pair. However, just at the point of being fertilized the egg discards half its paired genes, and the remaining genes of the egg and those of the sperm join together. Without this fascinating and unique process, each parent supplying *half* the genes, the puppies would possess double the required number of genes and the number could continue to double with each generation.

Chromosomes

At certain times, the genes can be seen to gather into lines or bodies called chromosomes, a name given to them because when stained they absorb the color and become visible. A dog, in common with other animals, has a definite number of pairs of chromosomes, microscopic structures to be seen only with a compound microscope. It is known that the human has 24 pairs, but the dog's number has not yet been precisely determined. Each characteristic in the dog's body is decided by the interaction of all the genes, but the difference in one pair can make a great difference in any given trait. Perhaps, this is easier understood if we consider that a certain pair is responsible for a certain trait. Let us assume for example, that consideration is being given to the trait of pearl eye in Pointers, and its inheritance.

Pearl eye is decided by the interaction of all the genes, but it is settled in the puppy by one gene given to the puppy by one parent and a mate to the gene given by the other parent. The main thing to remember is that each trait is determined by a pair of genes and not by one. If both are determiner genes for pearly eye, without doubt the puppy will be a pearl eye. If both are determiner genes for brown eye, the puppy will be brown-eyed. However, one gene might be for pearl eye, and the other gene for brown eye! In this case, what color eyes can we expect the puppy to have? To understand this, we need to consider the work of Gregor Mendel.

Mendel's Law of Alternate Inheritance

Even a novice in dog breeding will have observed that certain traits tend to skip a generation. The answer to this came from a scientist named Gregor Mendel. His findings came from breeding garden peas; crossing tall with short peas, smooth with wrinkled peas, and other opposites. From the issue of these "parents" he never got any type that was midway between the two opposite kinds; just one or the other characteristic appeared.

Thus, if a pearl-eyed dog is mated to a brown-eyed bitch, it is probable that only brown-eyed puppies will appear. However, if a pair of their brown-eyed offspring are mated together, both brown-eyed and pearl-eyed progeny will result.

Mendel, when he finally realized that tall peas crossed with a dwarf variety produced tall peas and nothing in between, decided that the tall kind dominated the dwarf, so he called the tall kind *dominant*. Because the dwarf faded or receded into the background, he called the dwarf *recessive*. Since brown-eyed puppies appear from the first cross always before pearly-eyed puppies, it is reasonable to call brown-eye *dominant* and pearl-eye *recessive*.

Returning to Mendel and his peas, he counted his findings and in the next generation found he had 25% dwarf and 75% tall peas. In effect, the recessives had skipped a generation, but it was a precise mathematical skip. Mendel bred regularly and continually, but he never found that his recessives gave rise to dominants, although those that looked like dominants often produced recessives. Later he learned that some of the talls were *pure* and these produced only talls, but others produced both kinds, always in the ratio of 4 : 1. From this he deducted that he had (a) pure talls, (b) pure dwarfs, and (c) hybrids, these last being "mongrels". The ratio was then 25% pure talls, 50% hybrids and 25% pure dwarfs.

Turning to the brown-eyed and pearl-eyed puppies, if we had enough of them, we would find then that there existed 25% pure brown-eyed, 50% hybrid (apparently brown-eyed) for the trait and 25% pure pearl-eyed.

Hybrids

The true meaning of hybrid should be understood. Many people think that a hybrid is a mule (the result of a cross between a male ass and a mare) or a canary bird with a finch. These are indeed hybrids, but *species hybrids*. A *genetic hybrid*, such as interests us, is a cross where a single pair of traits is involved. Thus, two genes for brown-eye do not make a hybrid, whereas a dominant coupled with a recessive trait, such as a gene for brown eye, coupled with a gene for pearl eye, do make a genetic hybrid.

The scientific name for a genetic hybrid is heterozygote (Greek *hetero*-different; *zygote*-yoke) which means a yoke holding different things together, such as a horse and an ox, although in genetics it means two different genetic characters yoked and working together. Thus, a pearl-eye gene yoked with a brown-eye gene, would be *heterozygotes.* Another name likely to be encountered is *homozygote* (Greek *homo* – same; *zygote* – yoke), thus, two things of like kind working together such as two genes for pearl eye or two genes for brown eye would be *homozygotes.*

General Genetics

Since Mendel's time, an intense study of genetics has been under way. Consider all the characteristics that go to make a dog and that every one is determined by genes in the germ plasm. Many characteristics of the dog are undoubtedly decided by many pairs of genes working on the same thing, even on such things as individual behavior, which would be a matter of simple inheritance.

There is still a great deal to learn in canine genetics. We want to know what all the inheritable characters are and how they are inherited, in effect to factor dogs down into their lowest common hereditary denominators. Many characters are dominant or recessive. In fact, Mendel's Law holds good always, but it is not to be applied to a single litter of six or eight puppies for it may not work; it needs a lot of progeny to prove its rules and ratio cannot be determined when there are only a few puppies.

Suppose you mate a lemon-and-white Beagle (recessive color) to a tricolor (dominant). A fellow breeder does exactly the same. Result: all the puppies would be tricolors because tricolor is dominant over lemon-and-white. When the puppies have matured, you decide to mate one of your Beagles to one of his. The puppies from this cross of two hybrids should produce 25% lemon-and-white. However, there are four lemon-and-whites and two tricolors. This does not reflect against Mendel's Law. There were insufficient puppies for the mathematical expectancy to be realized.

Individual abilities in different breeds such as "rabbit sense" in Beagles, speed in the Greyhound, body scent in the Cocker Spaniel,

Like begets like! Champion Luddecke Gay Lady is a great show dog and ▶ produces great puppies. TOM CARAVAGLIA

man scent in the Bloodhound, fighting ability in the Staffordshire are difficult to study and determine. Unlike eye and coat colors, for example, they are certainly impossible to decide upon when the youngsters are fresh from the nest. For those who breed with temperament and working ability in mind as the primary requisites, the main thing is to understand the principles of Mendelian inheritance and then remember that improvement and fine results are brought about by using only the best families, and crossing the best with the best.

It has to be realized that it is impossible to produce first-class features from a family whose heredity will not or cannot support it. What is not there to draw from, cannot be extracted. Only one outstanding puppy from a strain is not much for that strain to boast of. Conversely, the poorest member of a family able to produce uniform and good type puppies every time is worth the discerning breeder's consideration.

Mutations

One often wonders how it is possible to breed better specimens than the best dogs of a high standardized breed merely by selection. Mutations sometimes occur which render this possible. A mutation is a sudden change in heredity. More often than not its effect is deleterious - the animal being a throwback to an early and almost certainly unwanted type. However, the possibility exists for an improvement in some physical or mental and wanted attribute to occur. Such an advancement might breed true, whether a dominant or a recessive, and by incorporating it into his stock the breeder is able to improve on future generations.

Some improvements have come about by breed crossing and back crossing. Too often, certain breeds have been allowed to deteriorate. This may occur through the indiscriminate mating of bitches to unsuitable dogs merely because they held the title of champion, or for their physical beauty rather than for their temperament. Undesirable characteristics have been allowed to creep into breeding programs, producing shyness, cowardice and unreliability in varieties where at one time such weaknesses would have been abhorrent. Much of this failure is due to lack of knowledge, poor selection and the inability to recognize and capitalize on desirable breed features.

Fallacies

False theories, sometimes termed "old wives' tales", are still believed in some circles of dogdom, although with the huge development of interest in dog breeding, they are seldom encountered today. The following old-time beliefs are mentioned, not only out of interest but to refute their substance, should any reader still be in doubt.

Inheritance of Acquired Characteristics - False

Improvement in stock breeding was often attributed to the use of a stud dog in his old age. For instance, if a Beagle had hunted with the pack for many years, had shown great prowess on the line, or a Cocker Spaniel had shown great worth in the field, then such dogs were thought to be able to pass on their acquired and improved ability to their progeny. Many people believe that a mature dog is able to produce better puppies than a stripling. Such occasions when this has happened are coincidental, and were more likely determined by the health of one or other of the parents, or more simply, the individual breeding. It is seldom feasible to compare the stock sired by any given stud dog at either extreme of his life span.

Telegony - False

The belief was that if a pedigreed bitch whelped a litter of mongrels she was ruined for the remainder of her breeding life. It was thought that later litters, even those carefully arranged, would be marked by the influence of the earlier unwanted sire. Of course, such an idea is without foundation for once the bitch has whelped her puppies, whatever their shape or form, the matter is over and done with and she is ready the next time to be served by a fine stud and to have purebred puppies by him. This old belief had its useful side, however, because breeders were doubly careful to ensure that no misalliances occurred with their valuable bitches; this helped to maintain the purity of the different breeds.

Pre-natal Influence - False

Birth marking is another old belief seldom voiced these days. It holds that a pregnant dam is capable of "marking" her offspring through mental impressions. Pre-natal influences, such as being frightened by an explosion, are not impressed upon the puppies one iota. Neither can puppies while in the uterus be impressed into hunters or be acclimatized to the sound of gunshot even if the dam is hunted or fired over right up to the time she whelps. No, maternal impressions do not affect the puppies, but sparse nutrition, poisons, parasites, and matters not connected with heredity, can.

Masked Traits

Every dog is the product of his genes and the kind of genes he possesses render him important or otherwise in the breeding field. If he has a number of inferior but recessive characters masked by dominants, he is safe enough. But let there be inbreeding which doubles up the recessive determiners of inferior traits, then the progeny of that dog will evince the inferior trait. This is why inbreeding should be conducted only by breeders whose knowledge of its results is extensive.

Pre-determination of Sex

A lot of methods have been put forward by breeders for producing sex to order. So far, no certain formula has been evolved. Sex is due to the sperm cells belonging to two classes. One half possesses an odd-shaped chromosome called the X-chromosome; the other half has a full-sized one called the Y-chromosome. All the female cells have the corresponding chromosome of the Y. If an X bearing sperm unites with an egg, the puppy will be a male. If a Y bearing sperm unites, it will be a female puppy.

Sex is almost an equal division, with a very slight preponderance of males. It has been found that in cold months more males than bitches are born, but in the warmer months the two sexes come out roughly equal. Some breeders believe that they can influence the sex of the puppies by mating early or late in the period of heat. This belief emanates from life in the wild; a female shortage in the dog community would mean that any wandering bitch would be caught early in heat. Nature, being a great adjuster, would there upon set the balance by producing more bitches than males from such early unions. On the other hand, if males were in short supply, some bitches would go through their menstrual period either unmated or be served late in their time. This "Belief" is put forward for what it is worth. As far as known, its proponents have yet to prove it against the acid test of science.

Knobby knees and big feet indicate that these two photogenic puppies, if properly fed and cared for, will mature into large, sturdy adults.

The brood bitch should be fed smaller portions, more frequently than usual.

XI Mating

Choosing the Stud

Having learned something about Beagle heredity, and having purchased a good bitch, the time has come for you to find for her the right mate. This means you will have to select a suitable stud from the Beagles at your disposal, and this can prove no easy task. Nevertheless, if you have a bitch worthy of the best, you will take the trouble to arrange for a dog of suitable stamp and breeding, and then, no doubt, the puppies they produce will convince you that it was all worth while.

One of the old ways of picking a stud dog for a show bitch was simply by visual appraisal. Many of the old-timers, some of them illiterate, certainly without much appreciation of pedigree, knowing little and caring less about genetics, had what is known as "an eye for a dog". This valuable gift is an instinctive one, but it can be developed from a goodly amount of practical experience. Those who have it rely upon it implicitly, and there is little doubt that many great dogs have been bred by "instinct".

To those who do not possess it, the approach to mate selection has to be more theoretical. The old established breeding law of "like begets like" is a sound one. It means that if two animals of similar type are mated together, their issue will resemble their parents. This usually works, but care must be taken to insure that both animals are strong, healthy, and structurally sound. Further, their pedigree linebreeding should be pretty well balanced, one to the other. Of considerable importance is that there is no genetical fault in their ancestry. This is something not always easy to check upon, but with patience, it should be possible to conduct such a search. In all breeds, breeders with knowledge are still alive who can recall individual dogs on most pedigrees as far back as five generations. The avid genealogist may even find himself recording the heights, weights, type and style and ability values against the name of each dog and bitch whose vital statistics he unearths! Pedantic as this may seem, such information is of inestimable value when planning a mating.

It is usually found that when two animals of similar type and appearance are bred together, most of their puppies will conform more or less to the parental characteristics. However, an odd pup or two may turn up which does not. Say, for example, the parents are particularly good in legs and feet. This would indicate that the majority of the youngsters will have good legs and feet, but perhaps two will not. These two may have reverted to an early ancestor, perhaps one about whose weakness you had no information, or had hoped to bypass in your planning. It is clear then that in this otherwise desirable strain there exists a tendency to produce occasional specimens with indifferent legs and feet. Faults of this type can be considered teachers. It is up to you to learn from them in subsequent breeding campaigns.

When dogs that are dissimilar are mated, some puppies may favor the sire, while others will show the distinct characteristics of their dam. Still others will be of a type and size that falls midway between the two parents. It should always be realized that even the good pups will, when bred from in due course, have the tendency to pass on to their offspring a variety of features rather than specific ones.

The Stud Dog

Although dog shows are the pulse of dogdom and winning a championship is the aim of those who enter their dogs, the selection of a suitable stud dog for your bitch should not be unduly influenced by his show record. Some champions have attained their titles against less than mediocre competition, in spite of the fact that Kennel Clubs insist upon a certain high standard of adjudication at the championship events. By constant attendance at dog shows you will have become conversant with the appearance of a *real* Beagle champion.

In selecting a field trial sire, one should consider size, whether one wants 11 inch, 13 inch, or 15 inch dogs. Beagles have become fairly uniform by classes. A few breeders have specialized in the smallest sizes and enjoy owning and running 9 inch dogs. Even they, however, produce pups of the larger classes, but again, this depends on the ancestry; how many large dogs in the pedigree.

Longtime breeding for a definite height class eventually results in a uniform grade of dogs. Therefore, if you own an 11 inch bitch and know that the majority of her ancestors were 11 inch specimens, it behooves you to choose a mate for her which also comes from a long line of 11 inch dogs. Knowing what size pups the available studs produce also helps you to decide which to use.

Always choose a stud who is a typical Beagle. Substance and bone are essentials, but avoid a dog that is oversize; avoid too, choosing the very small dog just because your bitch is small and might receive him better. Small dogs are sometimes weedy ones, but in any case, they will frequently sire big puppies if they themselves are the descendents of big Beagles. Do not even consider a dog that is light in eye, and with straight shoulders. Bad mouths and wrinkled brows should induce you to look elsewhere.

Certainly never tolerate the indifferent performer. A Beagle stud dog has to be virile, eager, and able. When you arrive for the mating with your bitch he should have no eyes for anyone but her, and when he is released there must be no hesitation. Diffident studs are seldom successful sires; for this reason alone they should be ignored. If possible, check what the stud dog has done for the breed. If he has been regularly at stud for a year or two, one or two of his sons and daughters should by now be making their marks in the show ring. A young stud dog may not be able to claim such spectacular results, but judicious inquiries will perhaps locate a litter or two, or maybe an older youngster that he has sired, and these can demonstrate his worth as a father. Keep an eye on color. It is all right to breed most Beagle coat colors together, but avoid lemon to lemon if you can, as this often produces stock with dilute pigmentation, usually affecting the nose and eye rims, sometimes the eyes themselves.

The Mating Season

Do not mate your bitch at her first heat. She is entitled to a reasonable period of freedom from maternal duties and worries. The second heat is usually a good time to have her served, but only if she is well developed physically. Not only is it unfair to inflict a litter upon an immature specimen, the chances of her "missing", or having whelping difficulties can arise. The second heat is preferred because the bitch is then usually about 14 or 15 months old and supple; this renders her ripe for motherhood. A Beagle usually has her first heat between nine and ten months of age and thereafter at approximately six month intervals. It is only during this period that she can be mated. At all other times she will fiercely reject a male's advance.

The usual mating cycle (heat or season) lasts between 16 and 21 days, although periods of up to 28 days have been known. It is not possible to give a definite indication of the ideal day on which to mate a bitch, because individuals vary in their desires, often considerably. Usually mating can be effected soon after the colored vaginal discharge has ceased, The first "color" which is bright red usually lasts for 8 or 9 days, but in this period no desire for male company will be shown although the vulva swells and hardens. From the 9th to 15th day the discharge will lessen and become pale pink in color; during this period of about seven days, the bitch is "ripe" to receive the male, the top dates being between the 10th and 13th day. Mate her after the firmness in the vulva has disappeared, From this time to the close of her season she will gradually lose interest in the opposite sex, and finally resent any approach the male might make. Some bitches are different – they have to be "caught" at a certain time, often within a few hours. These are difficult subjects and need understanding. When it is evident that you have such a bitch, kennel her near the stud dog during her acceptance time so that she can be taken to him the moment she evinces interest in his company.

If the stud dog lives a long distance from you it may necessary to arrange to dispatch your bitch to him in a crate by air or rail. His owner will meet the train or plane, transport her to his home, feed her and allow her to rest. Later, he will introduce her to his dog and once the mating has been effected, ship her back to you. Naturally, in such an arrangement, a perfect liaison will be necessary so that all train or plane times are understood, and the bitch is not confined to her crate longer than necessary.

However, although some times such an arrangement cannot be avoided, it is not the best way. Too often, females sent off from their homes while in the devitalized menstrual state become distressed; frequently the matings are failures, and a lot of time and money has been wasted. It is, of course, the generally accepted principle to take the bitch to the stud and, if it is not too great a distance, it will be wise for you to go with her, especially if she is a maiden bitch. This accomplishes two important things; it will save the animal distress at being sent off to a strange place to cope alone with an unusual situation; it will allow you to be certain that the stud you want is the one actually used. This might seem distrustful, but it can happen that when one dog has failed to mate a bitch, a kennelman, anxious not to lose his fee, may either confirm a mating although none has occurred, or bring in another dog to effect it. Such an action could deal a serious blow to your planned breeding program.

If your bitch is a maiden, and therefore inexperienced, make sure that her mate is one at regular stud. He will know exactly what to do and be able to conduct the whole process efficiently. But if both animals are without experience you are likely to become involved in a circus! The dog will probably chase the bitch all over the place, and the bitch, at first thinking it's all a game, may tire, get awkward, and finally reject her suitor. When such a situation threatens, the mating should be attended by at least two handlers, one of whom knows how to do it. The bitch should wear a thin strap collar, and after the two animals have been allowed a brief run around courtship, she should be held by her owner, a hand grasping the collar, on either side of her head, to keep her from swinging her head to bite the dog if she becomes too excited. The other handler (the one with experience) should support the bitch under her loins, hold her tail out of the way of her vulva and with words of encouragement bring the male into action. The stud will know the routine once he is lifted onto the bitch's back for his instinct will guide him. However, if he appears clumsy he may need even more assistance, This entails directing his penis along a groove formed by the palm of the hand, into the bitch's vulva. Once he senses the contact he will thrust forward, then again more vigorously. When it is obvious that he has made a positive entry he should be held in place for a few moments. This will prevent the bitch from disengaging him. By this time his penis will have undergone a change. A gland, about half way along its length, will have filled with blood and swollen larger than a ping-pong ball. This locks the pair together. If the dog does not then bring his hind leg over the bitch's back, and back tail to tail with her, so that they face opposite directions, you should assist him into this position which is known as a "tie" and indicates conclusively that insemination is taking place. Onlookers sometimes inquire why mating dogs assume this position. It is believed that nature evolved it this way so that when dog and bitch are copulating they can defend themselves from both directions, as well as from all around the circle.

Once the pair have tied, they can be steadied, and either left to complete their task in peace and quiet, or the handlers can stay with them until they disengage. They should then be removed from each other's presence and the dog allowed some privacy so that he can retract. His comfort should be attended to by making sure that the sheath returns to its natural protective position. Both animals can be given a drink of fresh cool water, and some sleep if they appear to require it. As for the bitch, many breeders like to keep her from urinating for a while to prevent her from expelling any of the valuable sperm, but this fear is groundless, If the method outlined above is carried out sympathetically and with common sense, it is the correct way to conduct a mating. Some breeders prefer what they term a "natural" mating which entails leaving the pair to their own devices and trusting to luck that they will effect a tie. Sometimes the dogs do this, but more often they are found exhausted, spent, and unsuccessful. It is better to supervise proceedings because it is not unknown for calamities to occur during unattended matings. Beagles are valuable dogs and a great loss is sustained if one or both of a mating pair injure their ears and faces due to a fracas in the run, or worse still, if the male suffers a rupture.

One mating is usually enough if an experienced stud dog is used, since his regularity at stud will almost certainly render him "surefire". However, an unproven dog should service the bitch twice, the second service coming with in 36 hours. The first mating may well stimulate the effect of the second.

SALLY ANNE THOMPSON

English Champion Rossut Deaconfield Radish with a litter of seven puppies only 4 days old. The dewclaws are removed on the third or fourth day.

XII The Brood Matron

If your bitch was not wormed before mating, it is advisable to give her a good worming at the end of her season. The roundworm and hookworm larvae are passed on to the puppies while they are still in her uterus, through the placenta. It is important, therefore, that she be de-wormed and kept where she cannot become infected by worm eggs.

After the mating, your bitch should be treated much as usual, making sure that her naturally good condition and coat are maintained with ample exercise and adequate feeding, although her diet can be stepped up a little as she enters the fourth week of her nine week period of gestation, possibly with the addition of calcium phosphate to promote bone development in her puppies. Keep an eye on her weight; if she seems to be putting on too much fat, an adjustment will be needed in the quantity of food. It is much better to have a bitch in hard, muscular condition when whelping time comes than to have her carrying too much fat. A dog's normal gestation period is sixty-three to sixty-four days.

Two days before the birth date, reduce her feeding; make the quantities less but increase the number of meals. Staggered this way, her digestive system will have an easier time of it, and she will be more comfortable.

Whelping

Careful preparation should be made as to where the bitch is to have her puppies. Whether this be an outbuilding, the kennel, or in a spare room indoors, warmth and a suitable whelping box must be provided. The box should allow her to have her puppies properly, and at the same time give you easy access in order to aid her or arrange for her comfort. A whelping box is usually constructed of strong wood. It should be of suitable size, say about 30 inches by 24 inches, bounded on all four sides with low "walls", one of which will drop down, drawbridge fashion, to allow easy entrance and exit. The box should be slightly raised off the floor to prevent drafts.

As for her bedding, the natural whelping bed is saucer shaped. For the bitch kept in a kennel, fill her whelping box two-thirds full of some soft bedding material (not wood shavings), such as soft hay, straw, or dehydrated sugar cane, and fashion it into a saucer shape. This is the natural kind of bed. When the bitch whelps, the puppies lie in the bottom and stay together. When the mother lies down, she steps around them and lies outside of the pile of pups with her teats within reach. This is preferable to a flat floor where puppies are sprawled everywhere, some behind the bitch when she lies down.

If such a saucer bed is impractical, the box should have what is known as a "pig rail". This is a squared off piece of wood, measuring, say, one inch by two inches, running round the inside of the box about 2½ inches above the floor. The protection such a rail will afford the puppies is extremely valuable. Many bitches, having puppies for the first time, are very awkward, even clumsy, and this pig rail acts as a sort of "roof" to whelps; they can crawl under it and rest there in safety. Without a rail, the puppies could be crushed against the sides of the box.

The mother should be introduced to her new abode at least two weeks before her whelping date. If she is to whelp inside the house, her sleeping pad or blanket should be placed inside to encourage her to use the box. Of course, any impediment will have to be removed when labor begins. The best idea is to securely fasten a piece of burlap sacking or similar coarse material to the base of the box. Never leave anything there that can be scratched up to smother the newly born puppies; even hay and straw have some dangers in this respect. Some breeders prefer to line the whelping box with layers of old newspapers, as they can be replaced dozens of times a day if necessary and are quite comfortable for the bitch to lie upon.

Beagles are fair whelpers, but complications can occur. For this reason, a close watch should be kept on the bitch for the week leading up to the expected whelping date. Any sign of discomfort or odd behavior should alert you to a mishap; it is advisable to forwarn your veterinarian so that if anything goes wrong he will be on call. If the slightest doubt exists as to the bitch's ability to complete a normal birth, you must be present when her first puppy arrives. Otherwise it is better to leave her alone and not harass her. Most bitches whelp during the night and if you sense that matters are going well your attendance will not be wanted. When the bitch is near whelping, she is unlikely to take food.

The first signs of labor will be shown in the bitch's unsettled manner. She will be fidgety, scratching at the floor of her bed, turning around and grunting. When the first puppy appears it will probably arrive head first, this being the normal form of presentation. However, if it comes rear end first there is no need to be alarmed. Probably half of all puppies are born this way. Obviously, if the bitch is in distress help is required, but remember that it is best to give manual assistance only as a last resort. Natural whelpings are preferable, and if there is any thought in your mind that you may be too nervous and eager to help, it is best to leave the matter to someone else.

However, in case your services are needed be prepared. Have a kettle nearby filled with water ready to boil. Brandy can be close at hand, but it should be used only a few drops at a time - two or three – if the bitch seems to need it.

As the puppies arrive one by one, the bitch will become more adept at her job. However, if she seems uncertain when a puppy is half way out of her, you may have to help. Take a piece of clean terry towelling, gently grip the whelp and ease it out of her slowly in rhythm with her strains. If there seems to be an inordinately long interval between the latest puppy and the next one due, keep a close eye on her. If she seems to be getting more and more distressed, and perhaps three hours have gone by, it might be prudent to call your veterinarian. If the dam will take a saucerful of warm milk, this may help matters, but all extended delays are suspect.

Assuming that all is going well, the bitch will break the protective sac in which each puppy is born, sever the umbilical cord and clean up. She will push and prod the whelp around with her nose, sometimes roughly. This need cause no concern for she is, in fact, giving artificial respiration! Once the puppy breathes and has been edged around to a convenient position in the box, it will be ignored as the next one becomes due.

Between puppies the bitch may decide to rest and this should be encouraged, but watch out for any disinterest on her part, with weaker straining, when it is obvious that other puppies remain unborn. This could indicate uterine inertia, and a Caesarian operation may be necessary. If the Bitch's reactions are slow, some help may be needed in cutting each umbilical cord. This cord is attached to the placenta or afterbirth, which will be inside the mother. Take the cord gently between the finger and thumb; pulling from the point of manual contact to withdraw the afterbirth. Never put any pull on the puppy's navel as any dragging here may cause an umbilical hernia, an unsightly bump in later life, requiring a veterinarian's attention. The dam should sever the cord with a quick nip of her incisors, but if she fails to do this, it will have to be done for her.

SALLY ANNE THOMPSON

At first, make sure that the whelps are in feeding position every time the mother settles down. If one seems to have strayed around behind her back, pick him up and put him with his fellows until every puppy knows the routine.

Take your surgical thread and tie a short length firmly round the cord about half-an-inch from the puppy's navel. Then with sterilized scissors cut the cord about one inch above the place where you have tied it. Thus the cut will be made between the cord-tie and the placenta.

The afterbirths can be thrown away, although some breeders allow their bitches to eat them, believing that in the wild state a female would do this not only to give herself sustenance while incapacitated, but also to remove any telltale evidence of the whelping from the trail. If your bitch attempts to eat hers, let her, for they can do her no harm. It is very important to count the afterbirths as they appear. The number must correspond to the number of puppies. If there is one short, it is probably still in the bitch's uterus. If you are sure of it, call your veterinarian. He will inject her with *pituitrin* to dispel the unwanted placenta. Left inside, it can cause a septic condition which might prove fatal.

When all the puppies have been born, and it seems evident that the mother is reasonably content, try and get her outdoors to relieve herself. She may wish to badly, but some dams are so possessive that subterfuge is often required to get them to leave their babies. While she is outside you will have an opportunity of looking over the puppies to establish their sex and apparent soundness, and at the same time do a little cleaning up before she returns, when some warm milk should be waiting for her. Keep an eye on her when she returns to her box, watching to see if she is clumsy. If she is careful, you have nothing to worry about and can leave her to her own devices, but a clumsy bitch may need a little guidance to keep her from harming the youngsters. At first, make sure that the whelps are in feeding position every time she settles down. If one seems to have strayed around her back, pick it up and put it with its fellows until every puppy knows the routine.

After a strenous whelping, your bitch will be exhausted. Once it is evident that she is okay, leave her alone, preferably in a darkened room where she can be quiet and able to settle down happily with her brood. Do not allow strangers in to view the puppies. Stick to this rule for two or three days. Even your own family should make their visits to her short and infrequent, for she will thrive better if left to her own devices. If she seems a bit "off-color" or her milk is not plentiful, it may be advisable to have her injected with an antibiotic; not only will this rectify any temperature abnormality, but it will guard against her becoming infected due to low resistance.

Care of the Nursing Mother

The dam is bound to be loose in her bowel movements following the strain which has been put upon her, and constipating foods are in order. Get her back on a good feed as soon as it seems wise, but if her temperature fluctuates much from normal, consult your veterinarian.

If good, well formulated commercial food is not available, a staggered feeding system may be adopted for the lactating bitch, and six meals a day is not unusual. A sound and typical menu would be as follows:

About 7 a.m. Milky meal. Baby cereal and milk.
10 a.m. Shredded raw meat, lean.
1 p.m. Light meal composed of scrambled or poached egg, mixed with toasted wholewheat bread. A little steamed fish, carefully boned.
4 p.m. Milky meal as for 7 a.m.
7 p.m. Meat meal as for 10 a.m.
10 p.m. Milky meal as for 7 a.m.

The amounts will depend on the size of her litter. Extra milk flow to cope with a large family will have to be encouraged and supported by additional milk feeding. You will have to watch things carefully and gauge the amount and form of her food intake with the skill of a dietician. Patience will be needed, but later, when you see your bitch in the bloom of health with a litter of fine, healthy puppies, you will agree it was worth it.

Weaning

How you wean your puppies contributes largely to their future health. Badly weaned youngsters may suffer from rickets, mental and physical deficiencies, and an unhappy adolescence. The time to commence weaning depends to some extent on how well they have been nursed by their dam. If her milk supply has been copious, and of good quality, then weaning can perhaps begin between the third and fourth week of the puppies' lives. If the milk has been restricted, or if a big litter has taken heavy toll of the supply, it may be necessary to wean at the end of three weeks.

Dried milk products, especially formulated for dogs, are excellent media with which to start. Their formulae closely resemble the bitch's milk. Choose one. Instructions for its use with puppies, according to their age, will be found on the container. It has to be warmed to blood heat; a consistency of thin cream is ideal. A puppy should be started off with four teaspoonfuls of the mixture in a clean saucer. Put the youngster's head close to it and hold his muzzle to the milk. The average Beagle puppy does not take long to learn, and after a few initial difficulties he will start lapping. This food should be given once a day for the first three days but only as a supplement to the normal breast feeding of the mother. On the fourth day the feeding can be stepped up with the following formula: eight ounces of cow's milk, (or evaporated milk, two ounces of Karo or other corn syrup, with the yolk of one egg well beaten into it). A day or two later, scraped raw meat, or strained baby food meat, can be added. The mother frequently helps the weaning process by disgorging half-digested portions of her own meals for her puppies to eat. There is nothing to worry about if this happens. It is a natural function, but if it seems a common practice on the mother's part, make sure that she is not fed with chunks of meat, which, when disgorged, will be too large for her puppies to swallow.

When the pups are about five weeks old, the dam should be seeing very little of them. If they are essential to her for drawing off surplus milk, allow her regular visits to their quarters. At six weeks of age she should be separated from them entirely, at least so far as feeding is concerned. At this age they should be quite independent of their mother. They should be accustomed to a fairly wide variety of foods, enjoying their meals and thriving on them.

If worming has not already been done, it should be attended to now. Ask your vet to recommend the correct vermifuge for Beagles at the age of your puppies.

Puppy Feeding

By the time the puppy, now in his new home no doubt, is four months old, he will be needing much more food. Be careful not to overfeed him, especially at any one time.

Feed all he will eat two or three times a day. As he develops, he will need more bulk since he is putting on weight rapidly and forming his second teeth. This is a period when resistance will be low,

TOM CARAVAGLIA

Lady B of Lincoln Field is half field-bred, while Champion Luddecke Gay Lady as show dog is much bulkier and heavier in appearance. However, both of these have whelped fine litters with no complications.

and everything should be done to build him up. Bone formation must have attention so food strong in calcium and phosphorus with Vitamin D are essential. Calcium powder – about as much as can be mounded on a thumbnail – may be sprinkled daily on one of his meals – and a drop of concentrated cod liver oil may be introduced three or four times a week. Vegetable juices (never give ordinary vegetables to a puppy under six months old) are useful sources of Vitamin A which induces growth. Endive, turnip and carrot tops, rich in iodine and mineral salts, make an excellent broth to work with in guiding a young dog on the road to health.

Suggestions for feeding the young puppy were detailed earlier in this book. Good food, regular feedings, and variety in the meals will all bring a puppy along well.

SALLY ANNE THOMPSON

An especially large litter may require supplemental feeding. Patience will be needed, but later, when you see your bitch in the bloom of health with a litter of fine, healthy puppies, you will agree it was worth it.

When properly formulated commercial dry dog foods are available, they alone – along with water – can provide complete nutrition, and puppies will grow soundly on them as well or perhaps better than they will on home prepared diets which are time consuming. But because many dog lovers prefer to prepare their pet's food personally, the above regimen is suggested.

Hand Rearing

Unfortunately, it sometimes happens that a bitch will die before her puppies can be reared. This could be the result of complications arising during a Caesarian operation, or to an accident occurring soon after whelping. Sometimes a bitch is a "naturally" bad mother, or maybe too ill to show any interest in her puppies' welfare, or physically unable to produce a flow of milk. Whatever the circumstance, if the breeder is to keep his puppies alive he must take the matter in hand immediately. It is not an easy task to rear young whelps; a great deal of patience is needed; much time must be devoted to the work and often disappointment is the only result. However, if you can complete the rearing successfully you will have gone through a rewarding experience,

The makers of milk substitutes for puppies give instructions with their products as to how they are to be hand fed. Care should be taken to keep strictly to the quantities recommended and the correct temperature should always be observed. It is important that every feeding time have its "substitute" freshly made, and if the little family has a number of hungry mouths, it will be necessary to maintain the temperature of the food until the last one has been fed, so keep the cup of food in a bowl of hot water.

A medicine dropper, or an ear syringe, or a doll's nursing bottle, make excellent feeders. Any one of these can be easily inserted into the youngster's mouth to be sucked on. His nose should then be wiped off and cleaned with absorbent cotton. This will remove any milk which might dry and become crusted around the nose. Make sure that each puppy after feeding (or before) has urinated and had a bowel movement. If its mother were there she would stimulate these natural functions by licking around the anus and private parts with her wet, warm tongue and this would bring on a movement. To simulate this, take a wad of cotton dampened in warm water and dab the youngsters' parts with it. They will soon evacuate; afterward smear a little Vaseline or similar lubrication around. Avoid constipation at all costs for at this age it can prove fatal.

A hazard exists with the handrearing of young puppies in that the colostrum bestowed on them in their dam's milk within the first few hours will be absent. This substance furnishes antibodies against disease and for a little while gives puppies natural immunization. Therefore, to safeguard them, some artificial means of immunization must be found. Your veterinarian will know what to do. He will probably inject them with canine gamma globulin.

An infra-red lamp will be useful when hand rearing puppies.

LOUISE VAN DER MEID

American Champion Spruce Valley's Gypsy Hobo, a 15 inch Beagle owned by M. A. Foy of Maine and handled by Chuck Herendeen, a professional handler from Maple Heights, Ohio, showing an excellent front.

The temperature should be between 75 degrees and 70 degrees for the first three days; it can then be gradually reduced to 60 degrees by raising the lamp a little higher each day. The constant and regular heat these lamps impart is of vital importance to the hand reared puppy. Just as important is the temperature of the food and the regularity of the feeding. Concentrate on these, make sure that evacuations are frequent and regular, and you, too will be a proud and successful foster parent.

Dewclaws

Dewclaws are useless toes – vestigial remnants equivalent to the human thumb. Not all dogs have them. They tend to be inherited. Most dog owners do not object to front dewclaws but find those on back legs ugly. Too, they can be torn off or become ingrown. Dewclaws should be removed when the puppy is only a few days old. Better let the vet do it for you.

Champion Spruce Valley's Gypsy Hobo, showing how truly this dog tracks.
LOUISE VAN DER MEID

SALLY ANNE THOMPSON

The puppy should be wiped clean regularly to keep his skin and coat in fine condition.

Whelping Records

It may not be necessary to maintain records if you are a one bitch owner, but if you own a number of bitches it is essential. The record should show the registered name of the bitch, her date of birth, her sire and dam, breeder, color and markings, and medical history. It should list all the inoculations she has received and the date and duration of any illnesses. The actual dates of her heats should be shown as well as the expected incidence of her seasons to allow time for preparation of the matings. The date of each mating, the whelping date, and details of any unusual occurrence should be entered. The result of the mating should be shown, with the sexes, colors and brief description of the puppies, and the cash price they realized. Of course the names and breeding of each stud dog used should be shown and, in fact, the complete history of each bitch's contribution to the kennel should be recorded for quick reference.

TOM CARAVAGLIA

American Champion Luddecke Gay Lady, an outstanding bitch who, in the Westminster Dog Show in Madison Square Garden, won Best of Winners in 1964. She is being posed by her owner, Edward J. Johnson of New Jersey, who is also an AKC licensed professional handler.

XIII Showing

No dog can be entered in a licensed show until he is six months old. Many dogs are not ready, even at this age, to be exhibited for they have not developed sufficiently to be regarded as typical specimens of their breed. When this occurs, be patient. It is far better to wait another three, maybe five months, when the Beagle will have taken on enough substance and style to make him a force to be reckoned with in the Puppy Class. Of course, you can show him sooner if you feel that familiarizing him with dog shows will prove a good investment for the future, but with the puppy that has no chance to win because he is not ready, this could be a mistake. Far better to train him up to exhibition pitch by judicious application of stance, movement and atmosphere somewhere away from a show.

When the time comes for you to enter your well trained, typical Beagle you will find that you have a choice of two main kinds of events. The more important shows are "Benched". This means that pens are provided by the show management to house the dogs while they are not in the ring being judged. Above each bench is a number which corresponds with the dog's number entered in the show catalog. Visitors by this method have an opportunity to inspect each dog at their leisure; something they find difficult at an un-benched show. All championship shows are benched as are many of the big open and agricultural events. The shows run by dog clubs and societies for their members and others, shows termed "Sanction" or "Limited" events, for example, are not benched. Here the exhibitors with their dogs arrange themselves comfortably anywhere in the hall and enter the ring as their class is called to be judged.

Most owners start off by showing at the smaller shows, and many a big breeder today gained his initial interest in dogs at such an event, with a minor win. It is interesting to observe the way some people are bitten by the "bug" of enthusiasm. Some enthuse quickly, merely by their basic love of a particular breed or dogs in general. They buy a good specimen because they feel that a pedigreed dog should be typical of its breed and a pride to own; rightly so. Others merely buy a dog. Sometimes they set out to buy a specific breed, other times just a dog of any breed that is brought to their attention. If they are lucky, and this applies to both kinds of owners, they find themselves with a good one. A neighbor or someone with knowledge of the breed stops them on the sidewalk, comments favorably on the animal and advises them to exhibit it. In due course they turn up at a show and the judge examines the dog. He might award it a prize, or give them some hope by his comment that the dog will do well in the show world. This is the sort of thing which often causes the "bug" to bite.

Unfortunately, with some folks, it bites hard and they go about their new-found hobby in an indiscriminate way. A puppy or two are added to the first dog, money being paid out which the owners can sometimes ill afford. The dogs take possession of their homes and their lives; before long they find themselves saddled with me-

English Champion Rossut Nutmeg in an ideal show pose. ▶

CREDIT: SALLY ANNE THOMPSON

TOM CARAVAGLIA

diocre animals that need food, attention and veterinary care, with its associated expense. Their enthusiasm drains away and they drift from the doggy scene. Others, more fortunate, find their one dog a winner. In the show ring he takes rapid strides to the top, becomes a champion, and then other owners pay money for his services at stud. He gains for his owner some fame and distinction; lesser doggy people ask him for advice. Before long he becomes an expert and then a judge. Soon, the cycle is complete and this is the enthusiast at the other end of the scale from the indiscriminate one first mentioned.

It is those who fall into the middle categories who form the backbone of a breed – people who keep, perhaps, one good Beagle bitch from whom they produce an occasional winner, not by casual endeavor, but by carefully planning their breeding program. These folks get to know their strain, and their skill at picking the right puppy from their litters is proverbial. Such breeders exist in the Beagle world and they can be relied upon always to have a good dog at the end of a lead in the show ring. They are the ones to go to when a promising puppy is required; they will seldom let you down. Watch them exhibit and you will learn much. The know their dogs and show them to the very best advantage. Their skill in presenting the best points of the dog to the judge and obscuring the weaker ones is something to be observed. The art they display in moving their dogs is a revelation. Even the best of dogs when moved at the wrong pace does not stand out as he should. The mediocre specimen, cunningly moved to display ostentatiously his few virtues and to minimize his several defects, can sometimes win the day over a superior competitor. To achieve this with a less than superior dog is legitimate exhibiting; in fact, one might say that it falls under the show ring ruling which demands that every exhibitor should "make the best" of his dog.

American Champion Johnson's Fancy Dapper Dan. This is a fine looking 15 inch Beagle.

SALLY ANNE THOMPSON

English Champion Rossut Colindar Phantom, a beautifully bodied bitch with lovely bone. As we can see here, not all champion Beagles are black, white and tan.

XIV Sport with the Beagle

Licensed Field Trials are becoming increasingly popular in the United States. The National Beagle Club, formed in 1888, organizes and holds competent field competitions. Even before its inauguration there was a pack, known as the Waldingfield, hunting formally some two years previously. Although the first Cottontail Field Trial in America was held on November 4, 1890, those were days of lukewarm interest compared with the enthusiasm for the sport today. The rabbit, most common of the upland game animals, exists everywhere; because of this, and scent filled trails he lays down, Beagle-love has spread and been encouraged. Licensed Hare Trials are popular too, especially in the Northern states, and one famous pack is able to hunt the European hare which is localized near its headquarters. Everywhere a fine cameraderie exists and enthusiasm is such that it is not unusual to transport Beagles as far as a thousand miles afield to compete in some important event.

In relation to the sport, the following terms will be met with, and should be learned for their application in the field, and conversation at the trials, to make the subject of even greater interest:

ACCOUNT FOR: When killed or run to earth, the quarry is said to be accounted for.

ALL-AGE: Class for hounds of any age.

ALL ON: When every pack hound is present.

AMBLE: A slow pace.

AT FAULT: When hounds have lost the scent.

BABBLER: A hound who gives voice without reason, that is, when not on a line of scent.

BACK TRACK: To run heel or to run the wrong way on a track, to run to where the game came from rather than to where it is headed.

BAWL: Tonguing with a long-drawn-out note, with the head raised.

BAY: The note given by hounds when marking to ground.

BLANK: A cover or section of the country is blank or drawn blank when no expected game is found upon it. A day when the hounds do not start the quarry is called blank.

BLOODED: When hounds kill their quarry, they are said to have been "blooded".

BURROW: The underground home of the rabbit.
BRACE MATE: A dog competing in a brace.
BURST: Any fast part of a run; generally refers to the first part.
CARRY A GOOD HEAD: When hounds keep abreast when running the line they are said to carry a good head.
CARRY THE HORN: To be the huntsman.
CARRY A LINE: When hounds follow the scent well.
CAST: To spread out in search of scent.
CHALLENGE: The first hound to open on finding scent, challenges.
CHANGE: To leave the line of one quarry for that of another.
CHECK: A temporary loss of scent.
CHEER: A hunting cry to encourage the hounds.
COLD LINE: The faint scent of the quarry. This may be minutes or even hours old, according to local conditions.
CHOP: When hounds kill without hunting their quarry.
CHOP VOICE: A type of Beagle tongue much admired.
CLAP: When hare crouches close to the ground.
CLEAN HOUND: A hound without faults.
CLOSE HOUND: A hound able to deal with intricate scenting conditions yet keeping close to the line.
COUPLES: A link with a swivel-snap at each end in order to couple the hounds together. A pack is said to consist of so many couples or couple.
COURSE: To chase by sight and not by scent.
COVERT (or COVER): A wood, thicket or place where the quarry is sheltered.
CRASH: When the pack gives tongue together.
CROPPER: A bad fall.
CRY (VOICE OR TONGUE): The sound made by a hound when trailing or running his quarry. This varies in note at different phases of the case.
CULL: To eliminate unwanted hounds.
DOG HOUND: The male hound.
DOE: Female hare.
DOUBLE: When the hare runs back upon or close to her original tracks.
DRAFT: To remove hounds from a pack.
DRAG: An artificial line. Also the scent left by the hare on her return to her form.

DRAG HOUNDS: Hounds used to hunt an artificial line.

DRAW: To search for a hare in a given covert or cover. Also to call hounds singly from the kennel.

DWELLING: Unnecessary lingering by hounds on scent, i.e., when hounds do not drive forward.

ENTER: When young hounds are put in a pack, they are said to be entered, if this is their initiation.

ENTRY: Hound hunting for his first season. Competitor in any class.

FAULT: A point of poor technique.

FEATHERING: When the hound moves his stern from side to side with some verve, indicating that he has found interesting scent, but not in sufficient quantity to speak to it.

FIELD: Those other than Master and Hunt staff who follow the hounds.

FIELD, IN THE: The place where the hounds work at hunting by scent.

FIND: When the hounds first smell scent of their quarry and open on it, they are said to have made a find.

FLIGHTY: Uncertain, changeable; this being applicable to both scent and hounds.

FOILED: When the ground has been much trodden by cattle, etc., thus obliterating the scent, it is said to be foiled. A hare, doubling back on her tracks, is said to be "running her foil."

FORM: Shallow nest or depression in the ground, used by the hare as its home.

FRESH: The opposite of cold, when applied to the line.

FULL CRY: The chorus of tongue when the hounds are on a line.

GAME: The quarry.

GIVING TONGUE: When the hounds are using their voices.

GONE AWAY: When the quarry has been found and the pack goes away at a fast pace.

GONE TO GROUND: When the quarry has entered an underground shelter.

GO TO CRY: When hounds go to other hounds who are giving tongue.

HARE STAKES: A competition in which all hounds in a class hunt hare as a pack.

HARK FORWARD: A huntsman's shout or cheer to indicate that a hound has spoken, or quarry has been seen, further afield.

HARK IN: The term used to instruct hounds to go to another who has found the scent.

HEADED: When the hare is made to turn back, she is said to be headed.

HEADS UP: When hounds seeking scent raise their heads from the ground from the scent.

HEAT: A competition between a brace of hounds.

HEEL: Hounds hunting hare in the opposite direction to which it has run.

HIT OFF: To recover the line at a check.

HOICK: A cheer encouragement to the hounds. Same as "Yoick".

HOLD BACK: A warning to the field to slow up and not press the hounds too closely.

HOLD OVER: A warning to the hounds to keep to the side of the road.

HOLD UP: A warning to the hounds to stand still.

HONOR A LINE: When a hound gives tongue on the line of the quarry.

HOLLOA: The shout to indicate that a whip or a member of the Field has sighted the quarry.

HUICK HOLLOA: Shout to draw the Field's attention to a view.

HUICK TO (Hound's Name): A shout to encourage the hounds to go to the cry of the named hound.

IN BLOOD: Hounds who have recently killed are stated to be "in blood".

JACK: The male hare.

JELLY DOG: A British nickname for the Beagle. It arises from the culinary use of red-current jelly with jugged hare.

JUMPED: When a pack has been working slowly on a line, then suddenly makes the hare or quarry go away at top speed, the quarry is said to have been jumped.

KILL: Term describing the action of catching the quarry.

LAY ON: To start hounds on a scent.

LEAVING CHECKS: When a hound refuses to return to the place where he lost the scent.

LEVERET: A young hare.

LIFT: To remove hounds from a lost scent with the idea of trying to hit the line further on.

LINE: The scent of the quarry, indicating its track.

LINE HUNTER: A hound which sticks close to the line.

LOSS: When hounds are unable to follow a line they are said to have come to a loss.
MASK: The hare's head.
MEUSE: The hare's route through cover.
MEET: The gathering place of those forming the Field.
MOUTHY: A hound which babbles or is unnecessarily noisy is said to be mouthy.
MOVING OFF: When the hounds are taken from the Meet to the first draw.
MUTE: Describes a hound which does not give tongue on the line.
NOSE: Scenting ability. A hound is said to have a "good nose" if he follows scent well.
OPEN: When a hound begins to give tongue.
OVERRUN: When hounds do not check when they have reached the end of the line they are said to have overrun.
PACK: A number of hounds kept together for the purpose of regular hunting as a team.
PACK STAKE: A class at a Trial, where more than two hounds run together.
PACK SENSE: When hounds run together well in formation and honor each other's cry and the huntsman's encouragements, they are said to have pack sense.
POINT: The distance between two localities farthest apart in a hunt, as indicated by a straight line.
POINT-TO-POINT: A straight run.
POTTERER: A hound which idles on the line.
PUSS: Expression for hare (English).
PUT DOWN: Put to death.
PUT IN: Quarry which runs to earth ahead of the hounds.
PUT UP: When the hare is jumped from her form by the hounds.
QUARRY: The hunted animal.
RACING: When a hound goes too fast for the scent, overrunning the line.
RATE: To castigate a hound by whip or word.
RIOT: When hounds hunt anything but their original or "legitimate" quarry.
RUN: The chase of the hare from find to kill.
SCENT: The natural odor emitted by the quarry.
SCORING: The hounds are said to be scoring when they open in unison on a line.

SCUT: The hare's tail.

SETTLE: Following a find by one or more hounds, the others coming from different parts of the field join up on the line. The pack is then said to settle.

SINKING: Descriptive of a hare at the end of its tether.

SKIRTER: A hound who does not keep with the pack, running wide or taking short cuts.

SO HO: A cry used to indicate a sitting hare. A name acquired by part of London's West End, due to the hunt passing across its onetime farmlands in the old days.

SPEAK: To open or give tongue when on scent.

STALE LINE: A line which is old and over which the quarry has long since passed.

START: To find a line.

STREAMING: Going across open land in full cry.

STRIKE: To find or start.

STRIKE HOUNDS: Those hounds, that by their cleverness and keenness are sharp at finding a line.

SWINGING: When hounds are casting around in an endeavor to recover a line.

TAIL HOUNDS: The hounds at the rear of the pack.

TALLY HO: A formal hunting call. It indicates that the quarry has been sighted,

THROWN OUT: When a horseman or a hound loses his position in the chase.

THROWING TONGUE: When hounds are speaking or giving tongue.

THROW UP: When hounds have lost the scent and, in spite of attempts to recover it, finally indicate they are beaten.

TIGHT-MOUTHED: Describes a hound with inadequate voice.

TONGUE: To give good voice when on the line.

VIEWED AWAY: When the quarry is seen to move away from cover.

VIEW HOLLOA: A shout from a member of the Field to indicate the quarry has been viewed.

VOICE: The hound's cry or tongue.

"WARE RIOT" (Beware of Riot): A warning call to prevent the hounds from hunting any quarry other than the one intended.

WHIPPER-IN: The huntsman's assistant or servant in controlling the hounds.

WORKING A LINE: Following a scent.
YOICK: An old hunting cry, similar to Hoick or Huick. An encouragement to the hounds.

The reader will observe from the foregoing just how high is the degree of training required for Beagles in the field. Admittedly, the inborn character of the hounds lends itself to quick learning of field requirements, but nevertheless a deal of hard work is required before the raw young Beagle becomes the trained expert.

Beagle Trials

The great interest in Trials lies with the ability of the Beagle to counteract difficult hunting conditions brought on by varying atmospheric conditions or just plain bad luck. Both affect the success of hunting, but the able Beagle judge knows that eventually quality and ability will tell. No good hound can perform badly all the time, his worth must become apparent in due course.

Field trials run on cottontail rabbits see the Beagles run in braces, but when the trials are run on hare, the entries are run together in a pack. These are the two main sections of organized field trials and whereas we are mainly concerned with events which come under the jurisdiction of the American Kennel Club at which championship points are awarded, it must be recorded that many private outings are promoted by enthusiasts who care little for official recognition.

These official events are named Licensed Field Trials and a strictly enforced code of ethics laid down by the AKC has to be observed. The Beagle club which runs the trial will advertise its intention in a way similar to clubs which run beauty shows. Two judges will be nominated and their names, the place of the trials, and date with time of starting will be made clear. Any hound properly registered with the American Kennel Club and conforming to the required heights of the breed Standard and in good health and entirety, will be eligible to compete. There are two height sections involved in the Standard, one being for Beagles measuring not more than 13 inches at the shoulder, the other for Beagles measuring between 13 inches and 15 inches. These then make two classes, but each in turn is split into the two sexes, resulting in the formation of four stakes open for competition. The sport is quite inexpensive, the customary fee at licensed trials being $5 per hound, whereas

TOM CARAVAGLIA

The breeders of show and field trial Beagles in America have developed different types in recent years. However, it is not unusual for the owner of a show type Beagle to hunt him and to do so successfully. Many American Beagles with the Ch. – Champion – prefix to their names, bear the initials Fd. Ch., meaning Field Champion. Johnson's Fancy Black Joe is a valuable breeder, but given the opportunity and the training there is little doubt he would distinguish himself in the field.

at sanctioned trials, the fee may be as low as $2 or $3, with 25c charged extra for unregistered entrants. Bird dog trials are more expensive, of course, fees in these sometimes extending to as much as $75, but this does not concern us here. Since expenses are quite nominal, this may account for the steady rise of interest in the sport, which is the least expensive of its type; the main outlay as a rule, is transportation.

On the appointed day, a suitable time should be allowed to complete your entry form, which will require the following information: Breed, Sex, Name of Owner and his address, Name of Handler, Name of Dog, AKC Registration Number, Date of Birth, Breeder, Sire, Dam. These facts will be confirmed by the owner's (or his agent's) signature.

Your dog will then be measured by some properly appointed official who will use the measure of the National Beagle Club to establish the hounds exact height at the shoulder. There are a number of specially made devices for this job, the more popular being either a sliding bar moving at right angle to a vertical rod or bar-shaped constructions in wood or metal which are placed over the dog's withers when he is standing on a flat surface or level ground. These are made exactly to 13 inches and 15 inches so there can be no argument as to whether a hound conforms. All hound entrants *must* be measured at every trial they enter, regardless of the fact that everyone present may be aware of their conformity. Mature Beagles of 18 months or older, possessing the AKC Certificate of Measurement, will be exempt from this, but it is clear that younger animals may well grow out of one category of height into another class during early development.

Drawing for Bracemates

Once the entries have been collected, drawing will take place for bracemates. The method adopted for this varies. The collators of the entry forms will have allocated your dog a number against his name. The names will either be put into a hat or the numbers may be used instead; but more likely if the club is a well equipped one, the hound's number will correspond with a number on a ball which is tossed around with others in a wire bin and ejected or extracted at random. The first dog drawn will make bracemate with the second dog drawn, the third with the fourth, the fifth with the sixth, and so on, until all entrants have been paired. Should there be an odd number of hounds and one is left without a bracemate, this hound would be termed a bye-dog and he would be later paired with a dog chosen by the judges from an earlier run. The bracemate so formed would be under normal judgment when running.

(Overleaf) All hound entrants must be measured at every trial they enter, regardless of the fact that every one present may be aware of their conformity. CREDIT: SALLY ANNE THOMPSON

PURINA PET CARE CENTER

At field trials run on cottontail rabbits the Beagles run in braces.

Rabbiting

An appointed club executive will marshal a certain number of braces to a required position at this point. He will then hand over the first brace to the two judges and the trial will commence with the handlers uncoupling their hounds at the command to "cast". This will allow the judges a fair chance to observe the dogs in action while hunting game and to assess their behavior in the field. The beaters will meanwhile be flailing the brush until a rabbit breaks cover, when the cry will go up, "Tally Ho", and the judges will at once instruct both handlers of the brace to, "Pick 'm up". This means the dogs have to be caught and brought to the point at which the rabbit was sighted.

The cottontail rabbit abounds in the United States. It is a prolific breeder as well as a hardy little mammal and appears to withstand hunting pressure better than any other game. It is quite small by comparison with the British rabbit often weighing no more than two pounds. It is a great sprinter, and no mean swimmer, but has limited staying power. To offset this deficiency the cottontail is full of tricks to elude capture and often is able to set a puzzling line which can fool a novice hound. Also, the rabbit can hold himself completely immobile above ground, even with the hound nearby, ready to go to ground in a nearby hole or cavity if the hound spots him. It will be seen, therefore, that the cottontail, like his British counterpart, the common rabbit, makes good sport for the Beagle and Beaglers. It is acknowledged that the Beagle is a specialist in the arts and artifices of rabbit hunting at which sport he excels.

Both the hounds of the brace should be brought to the scent at the same time and laid on either side of the line and given the opportunity to hark in to one another, from which point they will be considered in competition. They will at once give tongue and trail the rabbit. At some point along the line they will receive a check, which indicates that the rabbit by some devious means has put them off the scent. Later, when they renew the line they will give tongue and continue the trail, until the judges are content with what they have seen of the hounds' behavior and method. The handlers will then be instructed to pick up, and the hounds can be returned to base; the next brace then gets its chance to run, and so on until all have been started.

After the running of the first series, the judges will convene to decide which hounds they intend to call upon for running in the second series, bracing them together in any manner they please. In order to determine the final winners, the hounds may be run any number of times in any additional series which may be desired by the judges. Careful assessment is made to determine the best runners in order to brace them for the best performance. Thus, although it might appear that the method used is one of elimination, it is untrue, for both dogs can be used in a later series, but two hounds who have run well together will not be run against each other should this occur; neither will two hounds form a bracemate in a later series if one has beaten the other previously.

An unusual rule that is exclusive to Beagle trials reads: "Before the judge announces the winners in a class, the placed hounds must have beaten the hound placed directly beneath them." This rule, like others which instruct judges, has been carefully formulated as a guide to correct procedure at the trials. It is important that judges should be knowledgeable, and that they are able to interpret the rules laid down – just as important as it is for a bench show judge to interpret correctly the breed Standard when he adjudicates. Further, judges should be impartial and Procedure 12, Section J, of The American Kennel Club's "Instructions to Judges", now quoted, indicates the importance of quality in a Beagle's performance over quantity:

> *"The number of times a hound finds game shall not necessarily give it the preference, but the quality of the performance shall be given first consideration. Ability and the desire to hunt are of first importance. These points are evidenced by intelligence, the method of working ground and the ambition and industry displayed whether game is found or not!"*

An important word is "desire" and a good Beagle should have this in full measure. A hound's first task is to find game, then to hunt it with enthusiasm and skill – all the time having a keen desire to overtake it. The experienced judge will never miss this attribute in a Beagle, for he knows that primarily the Beagle is a hunting hound whose instinct will drive him forward to perform as a Beagle should. It is the degree of performance which puts him above or below the level of his trial mates. Admittedly luck does play some part in deciding whoever wins, for adverse atmospheric conditions and other oddities which can affect scent, will detract from the work of even the most able hound. When conditions are so diverse,

SALLY ANNE THOMPSON

This is Canadian Champion Lees Glanrobin Little Buckaroo, a dog anyone would be proud to own.

it is certain that performances must vary, and the judge should know how to equate the chances of each hound.

The Points Awarded

Championship points for Beagles in the trials are awarded to winners of the All-Age Stakes. One point to the winner of first place for every hound started; one half point to the winner of second place for each hound started, one third point to the winner of third place for each hound started, one fourth point to winner of fourth place for each hound started. To be declared a Field Trial Champion of Record by the American Kennel Club, a hound of either sex must win a total of at least 120 points and these must include three first places in licensed or member trials. There is also a Reserve placing. This carries no weight of points towards a championship award, but, as the name implies, it acts to allow its holder to be moved up into fourth place in case that position or ones above it are lost by a disqualified hound.

It is interesting to record the points system of the early days of Beagle trials. Because events were then few and far between, only ten points were required to win a championship, although at least one win had to be made at a field trial that was rated three points or over; also only one win of a hound was recognized at any trial. Beagle trials were rated as follows: fifty or more starters, 5 points; forty starters and under fifty, 4 points; thirty starters and under forty, 3 points; twenty starters and under, 2 points; under twenty starters, 1 point.

Picking The Winners

As mentioned earlier, a Beagle has first to show that he can find game, then "drive it in an energetic and decisive manner and show an animated desire to overtake it." So says Procedure 4, Section H in The American Kennel Club's *Instructions to Judges.* Other rules of importance read:

> *"If competition is close, the Judges shall give greater credit to the hound that is obedient to the commands of the handler. A hound will be expected to maintain an efficient range throughout a heat and to show hunting sense in his work. Hunting sense is shown by the desire to hunt for game, the*

selection of likely places to hunt it, the method of hunting places, the industry in staying out at work and the skill in handling and trailing the game after it is found." (Procedure 4, Section L.)

This ruling indicates the importance of handling, and many points can be won or lost by the handler. The hound which interferes with the working of his bracemate will encounter penalization too, as will the "potterer" (he who remains too long on the line without progressing) and the "babbler" (the hound who gives voice unnecessarily), the "skirter" (who takes short cuts away from the line), the "back-tracker" (the hound who runs from where the game came instead of to where it is headed, or he who refuses to return to the place where he lost the scent). Such a hound is known as "leaving checks" and many other similar faults can be named which can lose him points.

Olfactory Sense

His nose is the Beagle's most important asset. This is a highly developed organ which will allow him to pick up the scent of game even when the trail has become confused. From one smell or scent sensed by the average nose he can select and savor perhaps five different scents and know which of these has to be treated with importance. Some claim that a very cold nose is best as it can sense and detect game under the most formidable conditions. The term "cold nose" does not refer to the temperature of that important organ, but to the dog's ability to detect and follow an old or "cold" trail. However, not all Beagles with cold noses are fast. If you own one that is, you are fortunate, and this is the kind you want to produce when you breed. Often a fast dog has only a mediocre nose, and it is important to *know* your dog so that you can enter him in the field which suits him best.

Nerves

A Beagle may be a good one, doing excellent work on his home ground, working well with his fellow hounds and with handlers he knows. However, put him on strange territory in competition with strange hounds and he appears to go to pieces, becoming ner-

SALLY ANNE THOMPSON

Large, longlegged hounds like these usually excel in Hare Trials.

vous, excited, forgetful and unable to put on a good show. Often the gallery of followers upsets such a dog and he works far below his best. This is frequently disconcerting to a handler, but such dogs need not be discarded. Keep them for local trials where they will shine and enjoy their work, and take another Beagle to trials that are further afield.

Some Beagles are quite the opposite. They seem to enjoy showing off to the gallery, and often go far beyond their usual performance.

Hare Trials

These make excellent sport, for the hare is very fast, enabling it to keep well ahead of the Beagles, often losing them. The hare, unlike the rabbit, does not check frequently and its endurance is much greater. In the United States, most hare trials are in the northern sections. Canada itself has plenty of hares, especially the snowshoe rabbit, which is, in fact, a true hare. The system of running the hounds in a pack instead of in braces has been mentioned earlier, but this is not the only difference from rabbiting. The hounds are each marked on the flank with numbers about five inches high, making indentification easier for the two mounted judges who are used for packs up to twenty-five, an additional judge being added for every extra ten hounds.

It is usual to arrange for three marshals to be present at trials, so the functions of assisting the judges, mustering lost hounds, and keeping the gallery regimented are efficiently maintained. The judges will say when the hounds are to be released; then starts a lengthy chase which can last for many hours, but at least for one and a half hours in the case of derbies (a hound is said to be derby while he is in the first year of his life and the following calendar year). In the case of All-Age Trials, the exercise must not be less than three hours duration. In practice, this period is often exceeded. As the trial progresses, the lesser hounds are withdrawn from the pack as the judges point them out until five are left. These are placed according to their outstanding work, the points being awarded like those in brace trials.

Under the existing points system, and with the tremendous popularity of Field Trials today, a Beagle has plenty of scope to attain the title of Field Trial Champion, and when he has achieved this goal he can be congratulated for it is no mean feat for any dog.

Packs of Beagles

Score of points for judging

Hounds – General levelness of pack	40%	
Individual merit of hounds	30%	
		70%
Manners		20%
Appointments		10%
Total		100%

Levelness of Pack. The first thing to be considered in a pack is that they present a unified appearance. The hounds must be as near the same height, weight, conformation and color as possible.

Individual Merit of the Hounds. The individual bench show quality of the hounds. A very level and sporty pack can be assembled and not a single hound be a good Beagle. This is to be avoided.

Manners. The hounds must all work gaily and cheerfully, with flags up, obeying all commands cheerfully. They should be broken to heel up, kennel up, follow promptly and stand – cringing, sulking, lying down to be avoided. Also, a pack must not work as though in terror of Master and Whips. In Beagle packs it is recommended that the whip be used as little as possible.

Appointments. Master and Whips should be dressed alike, the Master or Huntsman to carry horn, the Whips and Master to carry light thong whips. One Whip should carry extra couplings on shoulder strap.

Recommendations for Show Livery. Black velvet cap, white stock, green coat, white breeches or knickerbockers, green or black stockings, white spats, black or dark brown shoes. Vest and gloves optional. Ladies should turn out exactly the same except for a white skirt instead of white breeches.

The Hunting Folk

Much preparation – often extending many days – goes into the organization of just one day of sport. Certainly, tremendous enthusiasm exists and has to exist to make this possible. Landowners, farmers, and other property owners across whose terrain the pack will pass have to be visited so that their blessings are secured before the Meet. The sport is quite an expensive one. Apart from the livery required, the kennelling and staff overheads make inroads on even the deepest pockets.

The Master is usually a man experienced in the ways of hunting and hunts hounds himself. This is an important facet in the make up of an efficient Master for it brings an affinity between the Field and himself, matters being run on a more personal basis. This relationship should extend to the hounds too. The good Master must spend a lot of time with them in their kennels, getting to know them and insuring that they know him. This means actually feeding them in some instances, and taking every opportunity to teach them manners, so they will obey him implicitly. Sometimes, a good kennelman can be of inestimable help in aiding a Master understand his hounds and make sure they are steady when out. The inexperienced hounds must be prevented from sheep chasing and this form of exercise can reveal the hounds who are wrongly disposed to riot.

The Huntsman has quite a hard job. His task is to kill hares and while he has to conform in this to keep his pack up to scratch, he has a duty to the Field who want to see the hounds work and enjoy their day out. He is there to help the hounds when they check and the way he does this needs skill and patience. His method of doing this can endear him to the hounds and a firm bond will be finalized with the first kill. The voice as well as the horn will be used to good effect if and when it is required.

The Whippers-in, in spite of the fact that they carry thong whips, are at their best when they do not use them. Hounds do not like rating and the sound of the whip or angry note will do more harm than good, especially to the youngster out for the first time. Like the Master and the Huntsman, they need to know the hounds by name and temperament. Hounds are like people: they have varying temperaments and often need to be treated as individuals to get the best from them. The wise Whips will know how to manage them, and they will know how much more effective a wave or a whistle are than a "Holloa" in certain circumstances requiring liaison in the chase. A good Whipper-in is essential to the success of the Hunt; in fact, it has been said that a first-class Whipper-in and a second class Huntsman are better than an excellent Huntsman and an indifferent Whipper-in. Certain it is that experience in the Field makes for pleasureable sport to all concerned.

Beagling on your own

From the foregoing one must not get the impression that the Beagle is suitable only for hunting in packs and that most Beagles are used for that purpose. Nothing could be further from the truth! The vast majority of Beagle owners who hunt their dogs in the United States own one to three Beagles. In addition, there is an uncounted, but an undoubtedly vast, number of one Beagle owners who do not consider themselves serious hunters, but who do like to go out and stir up a rabbit. Beagle owners living in the suburbs who keep their dogs strictly as pets are often astonished to hear them doing what comes naturally – running rabbits around the grounds. To a few, this is an objectionable trait; to most it suggests a great deal of possible fun which the dogs can furnish.

Every Beagle can be much more than a house dog. If you are able to do so, take a Saturday off and go to a Beagle field trial club, introduce yourself and stay to watch the fun. You will see a group of men, and some women, really having a good time. The experience may convince you that a Beagle can afford you satisfaction which

PURINA PET CARE CENTER

The vast majority of Beagle owners who hunt their dogs in the United States own one to three Beagles.

you never dreamed possible. Beagle owners who live in rural or suburban areas, as well as a large number who drive out from the city, often have a favorite farm or open area where they can release their dog and follow the music he makes.

Oh, yes, it is music to the Beagle lover. The Beagle is a hound, and hounds have voices, not the least of which is the Beagle's. It is a thrill to follow the progress of the Beagle by the musical "owooo . . . owooo . . . owooo" as he puzzles out the trail and then, with the line determined, follows it in earnest.

The Beagle probably stands third in the hound hierarchy insofar as keenness of nose is concerned. The Bloodhound, of course, is first; he is without peer. The closely related Basset, who many believe to be a cross between the Bloodhound and the Beagle, too boasts a fine nose; but not far behind them is the Beagle, and his ability to scent is phenomenal. He is a natural rabbit dog and given even a modicum of training quickly becomes expert at doing what comes naturally. But don't think that this is a task or a chore. The cheerfulness with which he follows the trail must be seen to be believed. This is a dog which enjoys what he is doing. In the time of the first Queen Elizabeth's reign, many hundreds of years ago in England, there are records that the Beagle was referred to as "the Merrie little Hound". It has been assumed by countless people that this referred to his deportment in the home. Those who have hunted the Beagle, however, contend that it refers to his behavior on the trail. This is fun, and he goes about it in a cheerful, merry way.

For those stay-at-homes who own a Beagle, for those who own a Beagle and love to ramble in the woods and fields, and for those who are thinking of obtaining a Beagle, but have no experience in hunting, the following suggestions on cottontail rabbit hunting should prove helpful. Those of you who have already experienced the joys of hunting with the Beagle may find helpful hints to add to your knowledge of the sport. There is even a publication devoted primarily to the Beagle and Beagling. This is "Hounds and Hunting", 142 West Washington Street, Bradford, Pennsylvania, and serious devotees of this sport will be well advised to read it.

The Cottontail Rabbit

Cottontail rabbit hunting in America is not a shooting sport so much as a test of dog ability. There are those who hunt to kill and a far greater number who hunt to test their dogs' ability. Whether you like to shoot or to watch your dog work on rabbit trails, the methods of training are one and the same. Most rabbit hunters feel that for the dogs' good they should shoot an occasional rabbit. No Beagle should be gun shy but some can be made so if a shotgun sound frightens them just as they are becoming interested in their first rabbit.

If you want to train your Beagle, and expect to shoot rabbits, be sure that he is accustomed to loud noises. If he is not, he may take off for parts unknown when he hears the explosion of the shotgun, especially if it is close to him, and this will make him worthless as a hunter.

It really is not at all necessary to shoot in order to train him to be an excellent hunter. You had better start training your puppy at about four months of age. Get a fresh rabbit skin, and attach a cord to it and play games with it and the pup. Let him shake it and when he drops it, run away, dragging the skin behind you. The pup will chase it. You can run faster than he can. Run around a building and you will find that he will trail the skin by scent. Soon you can drag the skin while he is in his kennel and when you let him out he will find the trail and run it, probably baying as he does.

When he enjoys the fun and shows he is proficient, take him to a brush lot where rabbits live. He may find a trail and start right off on it. If there are any piles of brush, jump on one and likely as not a rabbit will run out. The dog will chase it until the bunny is out of sight and then follow by scent.

You may have a friend who owns well-trained Beagles who won't object to your taking your dog to run with his, This is another good way to educate a pup and many a Beagle has had no other kind of training. It is remarkable how naturally the good ones take to the job, almost like ducks to water. Yet there are many who are slow to learn and need special attention but who eventually make excellent rabbit dogs.

Rabbits run, more or less, in circles so they are easy to shoot. Cottontail rabbits run in the smallest circles. The larger species cover more ground and for them the larger Beagles are generally pre-

Did you ever wonder how the height of a dog is arrived at? With the dog on a level surface, the highest point at the shoulder is measured.

CREDIT HOUNDS & HUNTING

ferred. But early training on cottontails is a help and any Beagle trained on the little rabbits will run the larger species after a little experience. No one hunts the large rabbits unless he expects to shoot them, but cottontails, as I said, are more often than not, hunted simply for fun and to test the dog's ability.

Beagle owners who live in the city often drive out to a favorite farm or open area where they can release their dog and follow him by the music he makes. The cheerful eagerness with which the Beagle takes up the hunt shows that this is a labor of love for him.

PURINA PET CARE CENTER

AKE WINTZELL

The Beagle is a hardy dog, not subject to those diseases afflicting the breeds which have been bred to exaggerated or unnatural proportions.

XV Diseases and Minor Ailments

Few Beagles pass through life without some illness that necessitates nursing care by their owners. The ailments and diseases to which all dogs are prone are legion and this small book can not encompass them all. It is fortunate that the Beagle, being a strongly constituted breed, does not, perhaps, suffer from many of the ailments which affect some of the "manufactured" breeds. However, to withstand the onslaught of sickness, a Beagle must be well reared, well fed, and generally well maintained, and he *must* have had his inoculations against the serious virus diseases of Distemper, Hard-Pad, Hepatitis and the bacterial disease, Leptospirosis. Such inoculations are extremely important.

Inoculations: When a puppy is born, its mother's milk contains a substance known as colostrum. This contains globulin and has the effect of a mild laxative, eliminating the impurities which may have collected in the puppy during the period of gestation. The puppy is provided then with antibodies which will serve to protect it from disease during the first few weeks of its life. It is believed that colostrum exists in the dam's milk for only about 24 hours. A puppy that has missed this natural form of immunization (perhaps a hand-fed whelp whose mother died in giving birth) will need special immunization in the form of canine gamma globulin, a procedure upon which the veterinarian will have to advise.

A number of special vaccines have been produced by science to protect the dog. As these vary in their use and popularity, and even in their effectiveness in different parts of the world, it is advisable that you discuss your puppy's protection with a veterinarian who will explain the serious viral diseases to you, and advise you on the needed inoculations. The diseases of a serious nature with which every dog owner should be conversant, so that he can recognize the symptoms and act accordingly, are:

Distemper: This is properly known as Carre's Disease, after the man who studied it. Many years ago it was a scourge in Britain, whole Beagle packs became infected, and, there being no effective cure, succumbed. There are a variety of symptoms that can indicate the onset of Distemper. The keen dog owner should be aware of the normal pattern of his dog's behavior so when anything untoward is observed, he will alert for specific symptoms of viral infection. One of the initial danger signs is loss of appetite. On noting this, take the dog's temperature. If it registers above 103 degrees F,, the puppy should be isolated and observed, Further symptoms might be diarrhea, possibly vomiting, and a desire to sleep a lot. Sometimes, the puppy or dog seems to be "tucked-up" as though with abdominal pain, and there may be a dry, stomach cough. It is not uncommon for the neck glands to swell, and often the whites of the eyes appear bloodshot and congested with mucus. The sick animal will seem to prefer dark surroundings, being obviously distressed by strong light. Unless treated quickly the dog can develop a temperature of as high as 105 degrees.

Pending consultation with the veterinarian, the patient should be kept warm, not allowed any food, except an occasional drink of boiled water to which a teaspoonful of honey has been added. An alternative to this is a boiled mixture of 4 ounces of milk and 4 ounces of water which has been allowed to cool and then 2 ounces Karo Syrup added, along with the yolk of an egg and a pinch of salt; the whole beaten up thoroughly. If the dog appears disinterested and will not take nourishment, hand feed him with a spoon, pulling out the side of his lips to form a scoop or pocket and slowly pouring the liquid into it, swallow by swallow.

The worst side of Distemper lies in its after-effects and even if the dog is brought through the disease safely, there exists the possibility of Encephalitis (brain damage) or Chorea (constant twitching of the muscles, frequently in the hind legs, but sometimes in the head). Neither of these conditions appear curable, but the fits which sometimes occur after Distemper often prove only temporary.

Hard-Pad: This is really canine Encephalitis and is serious. The dog diagnosed as suffering from this disease, as well as Distemper, from which it appears to be an off-shoot, should be isolated at once. Its form is more distressing than Distemper, although the symptoms are similar in the initial stages. Some encrustment around the nose area can be expected and, occasionally, the pads too will harden and thicken; it was this that gave rise to the name of the disease. Early treatment should be the same as for Distemper, but your veterinarian will have to effect the cure.

Canine Viral Hepatitis: This is sometimes known as Rubarth's Disease. It is an insidious virus which attacks and damages the liver and blood vessels, often producing jaundice as a symptom, accompanied with complete loss of appetite, diarrhea and sickness frequently resulting in complete prostration. The temperature often rises to 104 degrees, but if you can get the patient through the first two days, the chances of recovery are good.

Leptospirosis: Two forms of this disease are known to exist in dogs, one being Leptospiral Jaundice (*L. icterrohaemorrhagia*) and *Leptospira canicola.* It is difficult to differentiate between them in the early stages, the incubation period being between five and fifteen days. The former attacks the liver of the dog and is contracted through contact with rat urine. This can easily be fatal to the dog, causing hemorrhage internally, and jaundice. *L. canicola* attacks the kidneys, the infection being carried in the urine of an already infected dog. Of the two kinds, *canicola* is the lesser menace.

Dogs so affected often recover after experiencing fever and depression for a few days. However, any youngster so affected can have the working of his kidneys and heart impaired, and this will shorten his life. Reliable vaccine is available, and this should be employed by all dog owners, especially those with dogs likely to encounter rats. Usually two injections are given in an interval of two weeks, sometimes one week. Unfortunately, chronic nephritis is a common aftermath of the disease; it can be combatted by feeding the patient a high protein diet.

It is only common sense when rats abound in the area where you keep your dog, that they be eliminated as soon as possible.

Coccidiosis: This is caused by a parasite, similar to, but different from, the ones that attack poultry. The dog loses weight speedily, shows signs of anemia, and often passes blood spattered feces. Take the animal off raw meat at once and feed only fatty foods in an effort to clear up the bowel condition. Kennel hygiene is essential because coccidiosis is a highly infectious disease spread by excrement. It is a self-limiting disease and given time the patient (barring complications) will usually recover by himself. Your veterinarian can provide medication to reduce the severity and duration of the illness and help prevent secondary infections.

Tetanus: Commonly called lockjaw. Contracted through open wounds, the germs generate a poison which affects the nerves, resulting in muscular spasm and causing very stiff action. Fortunately it is rare. To play it safe, any deep wound, any puncture or gunshot wound should be treated by a veterinarian who will inject antitoxin to kill the poison, and a drug to relax the muscles. The dog should be kept in a darkened room and fed an easily digested diet.

All of the foregoing diseases should be guarded against by specific vaccine injections, following the advice of your veterinarian.

Rabies: Rabies is an acute viral disease of the nervous system, usually transmitted through the bite of a rabid animal. It is an ancient disease, having been described by Aristotle in the fourth century B.C. Today it is virtually unknown in Great Britain and in some states in the U.S., mainly due to the strictly enforced quarantine laws; the incidence of it is high in India and the East, and not unusual in the Soviet Union. While it exists in the United States, it is not prevalent, and so far as human beings are concerned, the cases reported each year average in the twenties.

Stray dogs are a common carrier, however. They usually contract the disease from the bite of a rabid wild animal; coyotes, foxes, rabbits, bats, mice, gophers, squirrels, rats, skunks, wild cats, raccoons, opossums and muskrats are the chief reservoirs and diseminators.

The symptoms vary, but the infected dog is likely to show a distinct reversal of manner and character, with a propensity to snap and bite without reason. A rabid dog appears unable to drink water in spite of a strong desire to do so. The old name of Hydrophobia, meaning "fear of water", once given to the disease, reflects this symptom. We know now, however, that it is not fear of water that keeps the animal from drinking; it is his inability to do so because of his paralyzed throat muscles. This lack of muscle control is also the reason for the dog's jaw dropping and his hindquarters stiffening. While frothing at the mouth is sometimes a symptom it is not always typical. Many rabid dogs do not froth. So don't wait for this sign, thinking that the animal is suffering from some lesser and curable ailment before isolating him. To date, there is no cure for rabies. Prevention is the keynote. It consists of vaccination. In those areas where rabies is prevalent such vaccination is mandatory. In others – and your own veterinarian can tell you if yours

These are the spore forms of the parasite causing the disease known as *Coccidiosis*. These are shed in the stool, and are the method by which the disease is transmitted. Your veterinarian will make a microscopic examination to determine whether they are present, and he is qualified by training and experience to differentiate between the different types.

CHET PLEGGE, D.V.M.

Isospora felis

Isospora rivolta

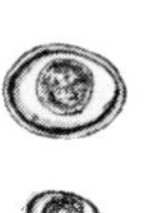

Isospora bigemina

Eimeria canis

is one of them – nothing need be done, unless, of course your Beagle is used in the Hunt where he will come into contact with wild and possibly rabid animals.

The foregoing are the more serious diseases likely to be encountered by the dog owner. However distressing some of them may appear, modern science has at least one answer for every one. The usual age for a Beagle to have his injections is at three months, although some vaccines are available for even younger animals. The immunity afforded is reasonably high, but full use should be made of the "booster" doses, to be given, perhaps, at yearly intervals for added protection.

MINOR AILMENTS

Abscess: A hard, painful swelling which can occur anywhere on the dog's body, often causing a slight rise in temperature. It can be brought to a head by hot compresses and caused to burst, the pus inside is then easily disposed of. The wound should be dressed with a mild disinfectant.

Alopaecia: The name usually given to baldness caused by after-effects of nervous shock, or of glandular disorder. Lack of exercise and poor feeding can contribute to this. If increased exercise and a more balanced diet do not correct the condition, consult your vet.

Appetite, Lack of (Anorexia): This is often the result of worm infestation in puppies, but it may be the symptom of something more serious. Check the animal's temperature and if this is abnormal, check closely for symptoms of viral infection. Always seek veterinary opinion if any infection is suspected.

Appetite, Perverted: Some dogs, especially females, have the unpleasant habit of eating their own or other animals feces. Occasionally, a puppy will eat coke or coal. The habit should cause no undue worry as many dogs are natural scavengers; in the case of coal eating, the charcoal additive can only be beneficial. However, it is possible that a deficiency is the cause; if so, it would be wise to increase the amount of vitamins and minerals in the meals. If a pup wants to chew give him large hard dog biscuits.

Asthma: This is found in older dogs, especially those that have been allowed to put on too much weight. Shortage of breath and wheezy breathing and occasional dry coughing are the symptoms. The heart can be affected. Your veterinarian should be consulted as he may suggest a change of diet or medication to help control the ailment.

Bad Breath: Halitosis is usually caused either by tartar on the teeth or an ulceration in the folds of an elderly dog's lips. The tartar can easily be removed either by scraping or, in mild conditions, by giving the dog a large marrow or knuckle bone or hard dog biscuits to gnaw. Where ulceration exists, deal with it by frequent swabbing with a soft pad of cotton dipped in a weak solution of hydrogen peroxide.

Balanitis: A discharge from the penis of the male dog. It should be swabbed and the organ bathed or syringed twice a day with a 1 : 5 solution of a mild antiseptic in tepid water. The condition is unlikely to be found in a dog at regular stud.

Bilious Attacks: The symptoms are vomiting and nausea. Temperature should be taken at once to consider whether or not complications exist. A sub normal reading or one which exceeds one degree above normal may indicate a serious condition, and then it would be wise to enlist the aid of your veterinarian. Take the patient off solids and feed him with a mixture consisting of a teaspoonful of Karo syrup and a tablespoonful of boiled water, giving one teaspoonful an hour. If necessary add a few drops of brandy to the mixture.

Bites: Drip a good antiseptic solution into the wounds with a medicine dropper, after having shaved the area clean. If the dog has been badly bitten, he must be taken to the vet. Snake bite can prove fatal. For first aid, apply a tourniquet above the bite if it is on the foot or leg.

Bladder, Inflammation of: This is an infectious condition and one requiring veterinary tratment. If the animal can be induced to drink copiously so that the system will be well flushed out, it will hasten the prescribed cure.

Bladder Stones: The dog's urine is normally acid. Should it be neutralized or become alkaline, a sediment in the bladder may form into small stones, some of which are liable to become lodged in the urethra and cause a blockage. When this happens, surgery may be the only answer.

Blindness, Congenital: This condition is, we believe, unknown in the Beagle. It is known as progressive retinal atrophy (PRA) and is hereditary. An animal thus afflicted would come from parents, one of which is either blind or a carrier of congenital blindness. Another cause of blindness is Glaucoma – definitely hereditary.

Bronchitis: This can begin with a chill. Coughing and wheezing will be noted along with a temperature between 103 degrees and 104 degrees. The patient should be made comfortable in a warm room; drafts being particularly dangerous, although fresh air should be introduced. Feed the dog light foods such as steamed fish, breast of chicken, broth, and so on. In severe cases a "Bronchitis Kennel" can be employed. Such a kennel is made from any wooden chest with a small hole cut in it. Place the patient inside and insert the extended spout of a kettle so that vapor can be directed into the box for the dog to breathe. The kettle should be filled with water to which a menthol medication has been added. Boil the contents by standing the kettle on an alcohol (Sterno) stove alongside the "kennel". The treatment should be given every four hours, but each application should not last longer than ten minutes.

The coughing frequently bothers the dog's owner more than it bothers the dog, and he will want to take action. A mixture of terpin hydrate, available in drugstores, is frequently prescribed to help loosen the phlegm. (See also *Tracheobronchitis.*)

Burns: First aid is to treat for shock as this is always present. Keep the animal quiet, giving him a teaspoonful of bicarbonate of soda in water and encourage him to drink warm milk in which Karo syrup has been mixed; fluid intake is of great importance in such accidents. Apply a pack of dry bicarbonate of soda to the affected area, or strong tea warmed to body heat, followed by a covering of Vaseline or similar petroleum jelly. After-care should include foods high in protein. When the burns are of an alkaline nature (lye, for instance), a 50 – 50 mixture of vinegar and water should be applied.

Cataracts: This is a clouding of the lens of the eye. It is sometimes encountered in older Beagles, entailing serious loss of vision. Surgical treatment has been successful in some cases.

Cat Bites: Most cats scratch and run, but occasionally a cat does inflict a bite that can be unpleasant. The bite, being of the puncture variety, is often a dirty one. It may be necessary to have the dog injected with an antibiotic drug like penicillin. In any case, shave the area around the bite and swab with a good antiseptic.

Cleft Palate: This abnormality is a congenital one. The roof of the dog's mouth is cleft instead of flat. The puppy cannot suckle properly as no vacuum is possible in such a mouth. The milk drawn in immediately bubbles out of the nostrils. Surgery is sometimes attempted but it is really a hopeless effort, and it is best to have the puppy put to sleep. The deformity is often accompanied by a hare lip. This is probably caused by a trauma suffered by the mother during pregnancy.

Colic: Intestinal colic is usually the result of indigestion, the puppy doubling up with abdominal pain. Gentle massage of the region will often bring relief, but a mineral oil or a mixture of half a teaspoonful of bicarbonate of soda in water or milk will alleviate the condition. Keep the patient warm and quiet.

Colitis: Inflammation of the large bowel, with diarrhea, some wasting away, and often progressive anemia. The patient will require extensive nursing, for this is not an easy ailment to treat.

Collapse: This can happen after a fight or accident. Heart disease or some serious disorder may be the cause. Recovery will, of course, depend on the cause. The dog must be treated for shock. Keep the head in a lowered position and gently raise the hindquarters, the dog meanwhile being on his right side. If the dog is *conscious* a few drops of brandy can be put on the back of his tongue.

Concussion: This could be the result of a heavy head blow. The dog should be kept warm in a dark room. If a hot water bottle is used, it should be covered with a blanket to protect the dog. Ice packs can be applied to the dog's head, pending the arrival of your vet.

Constipation: The cause should be discovered first. Faulty diet is a common reason – too much raw meat and bones. If so, the remedy is obvious. However, a more serious cause, a blockage of the bowel can exist, so every case of chronic constipation should be investigated. A simple case can be dealt with by dosing with a soupspoonful of mineral oil daily, or milk of magnesia, plus plenty of exercise.

Cysts: Interdigital cysts. (See Foot Care).

Cystitis: A chill of the kidneys often starts this complaint or it can occur in a normally housebroken dog forced to restrain himself for overlong periods. The bladder becomes inflamed and distended, and it hurts the dog to pass water. This is truly a case for veterinary treatment, but hexamine may be given in doses of five grains every four hours.

Diabetes: The dog often has an abnormal appetite and extreme thirst. The urine in such cases is light in color and analysis will show high sugar content. The animal loses condition rapidly, is often loose in his stools, and inclined to vomit. Let the veterinarian diagnose the case. He may prescribe insulin or a diet low in carbohydrates.

Diarrhea: Frequently a sign of some incipient disease. It is nature's way of disposing of the animal's toxic wastes which are upsetting his digestion. The owner should seek the cause of diarrhea immediately, for although it could easily be some mild upset caused by worms or rich food, diarrhea is part of the pattern of such scourges as Distemper. The dog should be taken off meat and solids immediately and fed solely on milky, sloppy foods until the stools have hardened. If they do not firm up within, say, two days, then the symptoms should be taken seriously and professional advice sought.

Discharges: These usually indicate the presence of some infection, and their continuance should not be permitted without attention.

Vaginal: This is common in bitches after whelping and it may be due to the fact that part of the placenta was retained. Whatever the reason, the effect proves very weakening and peritonitis can develop. All discharges of an unusual nature should be referred to your veterinarian without delay.

Rectal: This may be due to swollen or infected anal glands or the result of an infection inside the rectum.

Mouth: Teeth in bad condition can cause this, or ulceration in the folds of the lips.

Penis: (See Balanitis)

Nose: A dog perspires through the nose so there is always some dampness in this region, this being a sign of good health. However, if mucus is noted, it could be an indication of something more serious.

Wounds, Cuts, Skin Disorders: The discharge exudes from the skin. If the dog can reach the spot with his tongue, constant licking is the best cure. Give the area close attention with the application of a mild antiseptic; exercise and fresh air are also essential.

Milk Glands: This is sometimes noted when a bitch has excessive flow of milk in the nursing period. It often encrusts the teats, causing soreness. This should be gently washed off with cotton dampened in water which has been boiled and allowed to cool. Afterwards, the teats can be massaged with a little olive oil.

Distichiasis: An eye condition. A double row of eyelashes occurs on the lids, turning slightly inward. They brush across the eyeball and cause intense irritation. The treatment is best effected by surgery, although the careful use of eyebrow tweezers can be employed to remove the unwanted lashes; this, however, is only a temporary treatment as they soon re-grow.

Dragging Hindquarters: Usually a symptom of clogged and sore anal glands, although it may indicate the presence of a tapeworm. See: Chapter VIII.

Drowning: Artificial respiration may be attempted. Lay the dog on his side and push with the hand on his ribs, releasing the pressure at once and repeating the process every 20 seconds. Mouth to mouth resuscitation may be employed.

Dry Eczema: An inflammatory condition of the skin, commonly confused with Mange, characterized by dry, scaly patches, sometimes gray in color, that irritate the dog. It is difficult for the layman to determine the causative organism so veterinary advice should be sought.

Entropion: Either or both upper and lower eyelids turn inward. This causes intense irritation. It is a hereditary condition, reasonably common in those breeds in which breeders are trying to develop an eye smaller than natural.

Epistaxis: This is nosebleeding, usually caused by a blow on that organ. However, it can result from foreign bodies or growths in the nose. Ice packs will arrest the bleeding, but if it becomes chronic, professional advice should be sought.

Eyes, Weeping of: Simple conjunctivitis can be dealt with at home by using one of the proprietary preparations expressly prepared for its treatment.

Fits: Fits during teething are not uncommon. The coming through of the second teeth often causes pain, but this is only a passing phase and need cause no alarm. Sometimes, the aftermath of the viral diseases Distemper and Hard Pad will bring on fits; these will need veterinary attention as will epileptic fits, for which there appears no cure. The toxins produced by hookworms will also cause so-called "worm fits". These do not cause permanent damage, but, of course, the worms should be eliminated as soon as possible.

Gasto-Enteritis: This is unpleasant for both dog and owner, and if left unchecked can prove fatal. Diarrhea is a common symptom and the discharge may be spattered with blood which, if dark in color, can indicate a dangerous trend. Abdominal pain is usually present but seldom is a temperature rise noted. Stop solid feeding immediately and put the dog on milky meals, to which a small portion of honey should be added to soothe the bowel disorder and check the vomiting.

Grass Seeds: In summer months, these are a menace to the dog. He gets them in between his toes and often they penetrate his skin causing irritation and lameness. Remove the seeds at once, swab over the punctures with a mild antiseptic fluid. When removing a seed, draw it from the front of the wound, not from the back as otherwise small seed particles will remain to continue the irritation.

Harvest Mites: Small red mites which infest the fields in summer. Looking like red pepper they cling to a dog's legs and cluster on his ears. The dog will scratch and bite at his body. A good pesticide powder brushed into the coat will usually get rid of them.

Hernia: An umbilical hernia, which shows itself as a small protuberant bump on the navel, is fairly common in all breeds. It is often the lot of the first-born of the litter, especially when the dam, being a maiden, lacks experience and deals roughly with the cord. If the bump is small it is of little importance; in fact, only a few experts would deem it an unsoundness. However, if it is a large one, the puppy in question should not be purchased. It is a condition

This crossbred puppy has two problems. The pustules which we see are typical of summer Eczema. If your dog is kept clean, on clean bedding, you may never see this condition. Should it occur, your veterinarian can care for it promptly. The umbilical hernia (large lump looking like a walnut) is fairly common in all breeds. Your veterinarian can correct this with minor surgery.

which can be dealt with by a veterinarian, but it is always an added expense. The inguinal hernia sometimes seen in the groin of a bitch is more serious as is the perineal hernia which shows at the side of the bowel. These definitely need surgical attention.

Incontinence: This is usually found in the older dog unable to restrain himself for as long as he did in the past. It is common in the bitch, heavy in whelp, for then the puppies are pressing on her bladder. Incontinence can indicate kidney trouble too, and professional advice should be sought in such cases. When mature dogs have all their lives been clean in this respect, their reaction is often a worrying one. It is not fair to chastise them for their lapses; far better to put down some newspapers for them at night, or set up a litter tray in which they can urinate without feeling embarrassed.

This is an advanced case of Mange. Long before this dog reached this condition, he should have seen a veterinarian who could have prevented things from progressing so far.

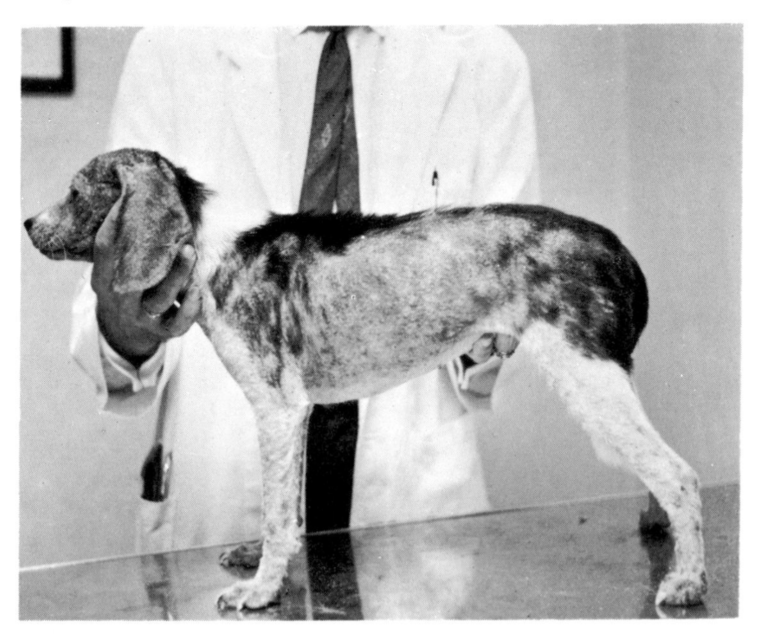

Later, when the cause has been found and cured, they will revert to their clean habits.

Indigestion: Often caused by over-indulgence or eating too rich food. The dog will experience abdominal pain and emit rumbling noises from his stomach. Withhold feeding for the day and give a spoonful of milk of magnesia in a little milk every two hours. This condition should not be confused with the distress sometimes experienced by puppies with worms. In these cases, the correct vermifuge should be administered.

Nephritis: This is inflammation of the kidneys, sometimes the result of renal calculi (stones in the kidney). In young dogs Nephritis is often brought on by a virus infection of *Leptospira canicola.* The symptoms are lumbar pains and arched back, vomiting, extreme thirst, and no interest in food. Vaccines are available to prevent the disease but they will not cure it.

Obesity: Many dogs on the approach of middle age tend to put on excess weight. This detracts from their general appearance, is unhealthy, and limits normal activity. It is particularly bad in the brood bitch, causing complications when she starts to whelp. Sometimes obesity is due to a glandular derangement, but more often it is the result of overfeeding, especially the giving of rich tidbits. If the trouble is a thyroid one, your veterinarian will know how to deal with it, but if it is from too much food, you will have to take the matter in hand, gradually decreasing the dog's intake by offering him smaller, carefully rationed meals.

Prolapse of Anus: This is common in small puppies after straining either from constipation or worm infection. The prolapsed rectum can easily be replaced, under anaesthetic, by your veterinarian.

Rickets: This was a common condition some years ago but it is seldom encountered today because of our more enlightened methods of dog breeding, and the availability of foods correctly balanced in calcium, phosphorus and Vitamin D. Sometimes a bitch in poor health will produce ricketty puppies. Their joints will be found enlarged, particularly at the knees, hocks and stifles. There will be a tendency to walk on the hocks and sometimes curvature of the spine is evident. Even with correct feeding and extended care, this condition will never really disappear, even with maturity, but it can be eased by feeding the animal a good complete dog food. All of the better grades of dog food now on the market contain every nutritional element necessary to grow "unricketty" dogs.

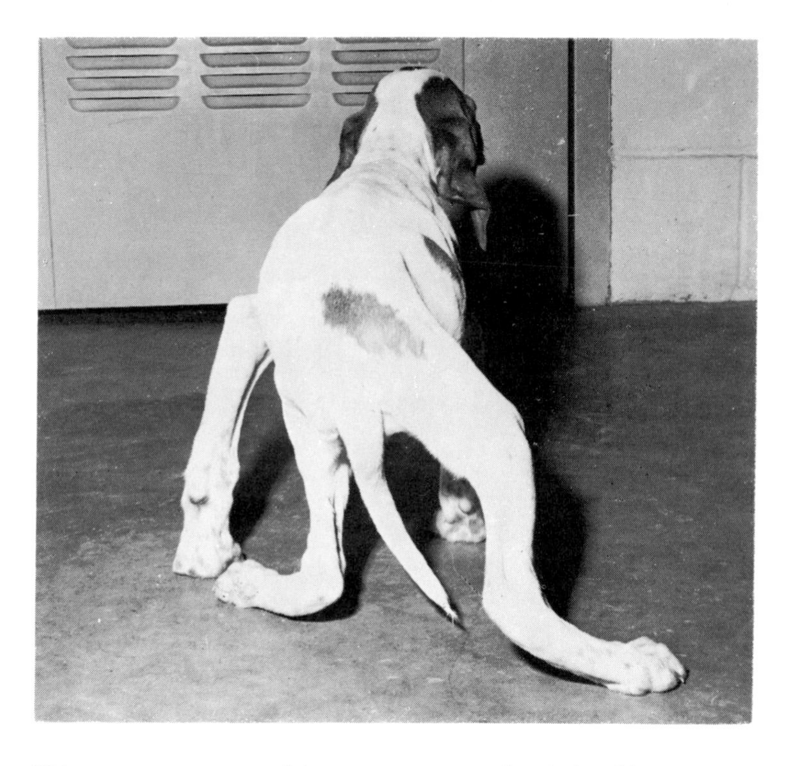

This was a common condition some years ago but it is seldom encountered today because of our more enlightened methods of breeding and feeding. This Pointer puppy received a low calcium diet, resulting in the distortions which we see here.

Skin Troubles: There are a variety of these, and while they are frequently lumped together as "Mange" they include Ringworm, Eczema, and Ear Canker which we discussed in the chapter on Grooming.

Ringworm: Ringworm is not a worm but a fungus. It is characterized by ring-shaped discolored patches on the skin. Since it affects human beings as well as animals, always be extremely cautious when treating an infected dog. Let the veterinarian diagnose and prescribe. Let me say it now, if I haven't already, that in all skin ailments the symptoms are superficially the same and, since some of them are much more dangerous than others, professional treatment is always the wiser course.

Demodex folliculorum

CHET PLEGGE, D.V.M.

Demodex folliculorum. It is this mite, burrowing into the skin of the dog, which causes Demodectic or Red Mange.

Follicular Mange: This is sometimes known as demodectic mange, or red mange because of the raw, dark red patches. It is not easy to cure and short-coated breeds like the Beagle seem more prone to it than do long-coated varieties.

The first signs of trouble usually appear on the cheeks, skull, side of the neck, or on the lower legs, although they can appear anywhere. The spots usually start off the size of a postage stamp but they gradually increase in size and join up with neighboring patches. At first, there appears no irritation but as the disease progresses inflammation sets in, causing the dog distress. This, coupled with the enervating effect of the poisons produced by the mites, undermines the dog's health and, on occasion, death is the result. However, if the disease is discovered in time and properly treated, the dog can be brought back to normal coat and good health. There are a number of commercially prepared medications on the market, available at pet shops. Your best course, if you suspect that your dog has red mange, is to see your vet.

Sarcoptic Mange: The mites that cause this are about 1/100th of an inch long. It is similar to but not the same as the skin trouble which affects humans, and is known as "scabies", the word coming from the formation of scabs. The disease resembles dry eczema, usually starting between the eyes or below the ears. Pustules form and emit a discharge which encrusts, causing the dog intense discomfort. Sulphur ointment treatment has been found effective in combatting the scourge which if not dealt with quickly can have serious results. It has been known to cause digestive troubles, and to lower the patient's vitality.

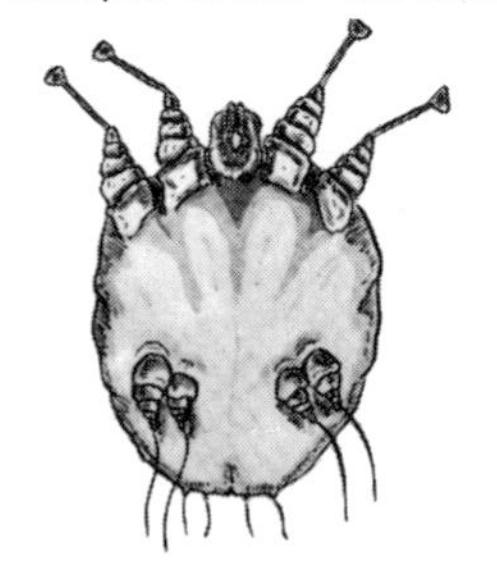

CHET PLEGGE, D.V.M.

Sarcoptes scabiei – Var. canis. This mite, in the skin of the dog, causes Sarcoptic Mange. Should your veterinarian suspect Mange, he will scrape the dog's skin and examine the scrapings in a drop of oil under a microscope.

As with skin disorders in humans, those of dogs are often misinterpreted in diagnosis. Frequently a microscope is needed to determine their cause. Whenever you have a dog affected by one of the "manges", your first move should be to make him healthy *inside* and then attack the outside. Exercise, fresh air and the judicious application of conditioning food supplements are of vital importance. Conditions diagnosed as follicular mange have been cured quickly with thyroid glandular treatment; sarcoptic mange has made a speedy exit after a few massages of chicken, kerosene, or lard. With all manges, experimentation is advised – even some of the old wives' recipes should not be discarded out of hand.

Temperature: The dog's normal temperature is 101 tot 102.2°F. and if it goes higher than that and stays high for 24 hours, consider it a danger signal. A dog's temperature is taken with a rectal thermometer greased with Vaseline and inserted in the rectum for about two inches and left there for at least a minute.

Tonsilitis: An inflammatory condition of the tonsils caused by virus or bacteria. The presence of bacteria can be determined from throat swabs examined in the laboratory. The veterinarian will then know what antibiotic to prescribe to clear up the condition promptly. The dog will show symptoms of lassitude, lack of appetite, and experience a very sore throat along with a rough cough. The condition is infectious and a dog with tonsilitis should be isolated from his kennel mates. Antibiotic treatment will usually cure the condition if it is not due to some virus. The removal of the tonsils in chronic cases should be considered only as a last resort.

Tracheobronchitis: Usually called "Kennel Cough", this is a common ailment of puppies. It is characterized by a dry gagging cough that is usually more severe at night. In every other respect – even temperature – the puppy appears to be perfectly normal. Fortunately, Kennel Cough is a self-limiting disease; this means that the dog usually recovers without treatment. There are cough syrups available to ease his raw throat, or a child's cough syrup may be used. For severe cases, consult your vet. He will probably prescribe an antibiotic.

A good spray is probably the most convenient method of disposing of fleas, lice and ticks.

SALLY ANNE THOMPSON

Urticaria: This is nettle rash. The skin comes up in welts or lumps, and swelling occurs in other parts of the body, causing the dog intense discomfort. It can be caused by the dog's allergy to some particular drug: many dogs react thus to penicillin, just as do some humans. The eyes should be bathed in boric acid and the body swabbed with a weak solution of baking soda and water. In advanced cases, an injection of adrenalin will give relief. If the dog has collapsed, a strong mixture of Karo syrup and water should be poured in small swallows into a pocket formed by pulling out the lips.

Ctenocephalides canis

CHET PLEGGE, D.V.M.

Ctenocephalides canis. This is a common dog flea. In spite of what some people have said, he actually does prefer dogs to humans.

Wasp Stings: These and bee stings can prove dangerous. Dogs are inclined to poke their noses at the insects, sometimes snap them into their mouths with disastrous results. Alternately, a dog will paw at one. In either case he is likely to get stung. In the wasp season it is a good idea to have a wide necked jar of a strong solution of bicarbonate of soda (two tablespoonsful to a pint of water) handy. As soon as a sting is noted it should be liberally swabbed with solution; if a foot has been stung, put the entire foot into the jar. Another method is to rub the spot with a lump of ordinary washing soda, or to dab on a good antiseptic.

Fleas: Most dogs pick up an occasional flea, either from other dogs or from grass and hedgerows through which other animals have traveled. One of the main offenders for distributing fleas is the hedgehog; chickens, too, are notable hosts. Fleas are tiny black insects which hide in the dog's coat, a common hideout being the set-on of the tail. If the hair is parted quickly, they will dart at once into another part of the coat, being capable of great leaps. Their bites when detected look rather like mosquito bites. Both male and female fleas invade the dog's coat, the female's eggs falling off to the ground where they hatch; the youngsters then tack themselves on to any passing animal. Pet shops stock many effective flea killers. Remember that not only should the dog be treated, but also his bedding and, for safety's sake, all surrounding areas so that any newly hatched fleas are disposed of at the same time. Fleas are particularly dangerous to dogs for they are known to be the intermediate hosts of the tapeworm.

The most effective flea control consists of using the 90 day dog collar.* When worn around the dog's neck, the collar eliminates fleas everywhere on your pet for three full months.

Lice: There are two types of lice – biting and sucking. Both kinds spend their whole life cycle on their host. Unlike the flea, they lay their eggs on the animal. These the female attaches to individual hairs where they can usually be detected. Known as nits, they usually take from five to twelve days to hatch, depending on the variety. Pesticide powders and sprays, obtainable at pet shops, will keep the lice down but to rid the dog of them permanently entails a series of disinfecting baths. These should be given at ten day intervals to dispose of both lice and nits.

Ticks: There are many kinds of ticks but they are all bloodsuckers, fastening themselves to the skin of the animal and engorging its blood. Usually picked up in the woods and fields, ticks range in size from a pea down to a pinhead, the color being light gray or light green. These are the British kind. In America, there are two common sorts, one the Brown Dog Tick, the other the American Dog Tick. The Brown Dog Tick infests buildings, the other prefers the fields. Only the female is parasitic; the male lives under her inflated body. She attaches herself by means of sucking pincers to the dog's skin. As she sucks blood she swells to the size of a small grape. When replete she drops off her host in some quiet spot, lays some 6,000 eggs and dies. These hatch, go through several stages, and when mature crawl up plants and bushes to a height about a foot from the ground. There they lay in wait for some passing animal to fasten onto.

When ticks are discovered on the dog, do not just pull them off or you will leave the female's sucking pincers in the skin, and the incision is likely to fester. The right way is to drop a spot of euca-

* Trade mark.

lyptus oil, turpentine, camphor, or alcohol onto the tick; it will loosen its grip and can then be lifted off with tweezers. Destroy the tick at once, otherwise it will attach itself to another host.

The Brown Dog Tick prefers to infest houses (it is frequently carried in on house plants) but confines its attentions to dogs and cats, not humans. It is an unpleasant visitor, for once established a vermin exterminator may be needed to dispose of it.

Worms: Almost every dog is infected with worms at some time in his life. They are prevalent in puppies – many times they are contracted from their mother before they are born. Worms usually develop from eggs passed in dog stools. Other dogs sniff at the stools, get the eggs on their muzzles, lick them off and swallow them. They then incubate in the digestive tract. Worm eggs can be brought into the house or kennel on the soles of shoes or embedded in the dog's foot pads. Cleanliness in dog keeping is essential, and regular disinfection of your dog's quarters will keep down worm infestation. Once it has been established that a dog has worms they should be eliminated immediately. Bad infestations can result in death.

Worm symptoms: Some of the more common symptoms – aside from the actual appearance of the worm or worm segments in feces or vomit – include a "potbelly", diarrhea, persistent vomiting, and runny (but not mucousy) eyes and nose. Worms can cause coughing and when they get into the lungs, wheezing. These latter symptoms last only a few days, however. Dragging the rump on the floor is sometimes an indication but it usually means that there is an accumulation of impacted matter in the dog's anal glands (See: Grooming).

Dispelling worms is not difficult, the most important factor being diagnosis as to the variety of worm. This can be established by your veterinarian who will take a sample of the dog's stool and examine it for eggs under his microscope.

The following are the various kinds of worms likely to be encountered:

Roundworm: Commonly found in puppies of all breeds, roundworms have been known to cause death in very young dogs, especially those reared carelessly that have developed little resistance. This is a worm with which most dog owners are familiar. It is fairly long, of a yellowish, pinky color, and vermicelli-like in appearance. Roundworm larvae will infest the bloodstream of the in-whelp bitch and can be passed to her young through the placentae. Most breeders, to prevent this, worm the bitch in the early days of her gestation; and then worm the young pups when two or three weeks old. This seems to me to be a somewhat risky business unless performed by a person who knows what he's doing; a worming later – say, at around five weeks of age, is much safer. There are many first-class vermifuges on the market but better let your vet prescribe.

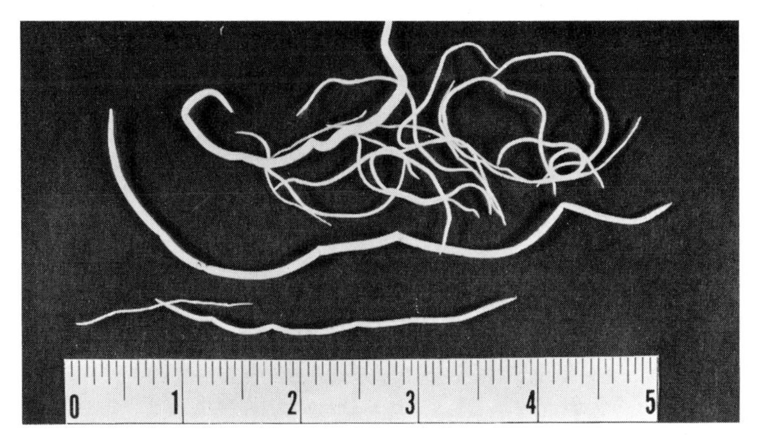

PURINA PET CARE CENTER

Roundworms. This is one of the most common parasites in dogs.

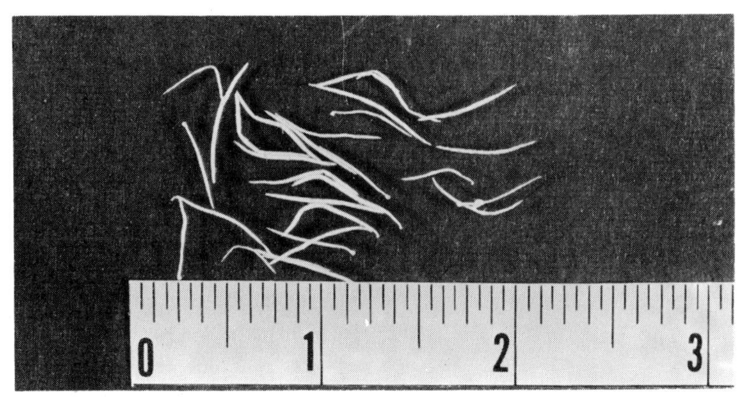

PURINA PET CARE CENTER

Hookworms. These are the most injurious internal parasites in puppies. They are thin as a thread and about half an inch long.

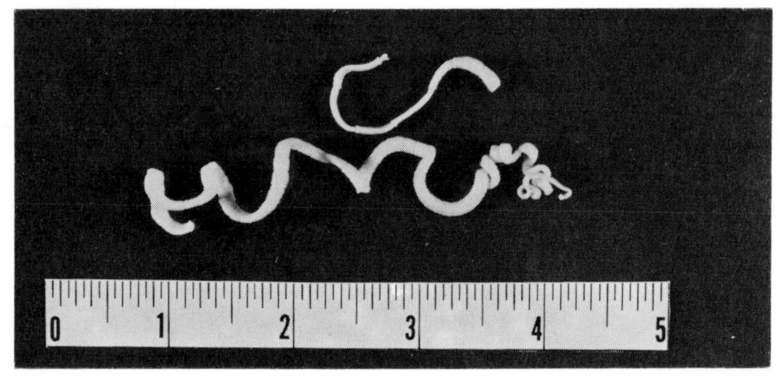

PURINA PET CARE CENTER

Frequently the segments of the Tapeworm may be seen in the dog's movement, looking like rice grains.

Whipworm: These are seldom if ever found in very young puppies; they prefer youngsters three months of age and older. Common enough in the warmer southern states, whipworms incubate in the soil for about six weeks during warm weather although they appear resistant to freezing. When the egg is swallowed by an animal, the parasite hatches and makes its home in the intestine. Often his breath will be bad and his skin emit an unpleasant smell. In view of the possibility of infection from the flea, the dog should be checked regularly. There are several effective drugs available, one of which your vet will prescribe.

Administering Medicine: On no account should the dog's mouth be opened wide and liquid poured haphazardly down his throat. It can enter his windpipe and choke him. The best method is to hold his mouth closed with the head raised. Put a forefinger between his lips at the side of his mouth, pulling them out to form a sort of scoop or pocket. Pour the liquid into this pocket in small doses, allowing the dog to swallow each time. If the dog is restless, an assistant can help. A dog will take some medicines right from a spoon or when they are mixed with some tasty bit of food. However, it is best to administer medicine directly so you know that it has been imbibed.

Pills and tablets are easy to give. Open the dog's jaws and poke the pill as far back down his throat as you can with the index and middle fingers. You will know it has gone down when he swallows, but to make sure gently massage his throat.

AKE WINTZELL

When the Beagle is on the trail, he concentrates on his work to the exclusion of all else. It is at times like these that he can be cut or injured, often seemingly without his being aware of it. Therefore, it is important at the end of each hunt that the dog be examined carefully, paying particular attention to the eyes and the pads.

XVI First Aid

One never knows when it will become necessary to render useful and comforting assistance to a dog in an emergency. Whether it is your own dog in trouble or a strange dog in the street which has been hit by an automobile, it is a good thing to be prepared. First aid is initial emergency treatment. It should be given to relieve the animal's pain, and to keep him as quiet and comfortable as possible until professional veterinary assistance can come to his aid.

Restraining an Injured Dog

Any dog, even your own, can forget the bond of trust when he is suffering from the pain and shock of an accident. The best natured

Dog wearing Elizabethan collar

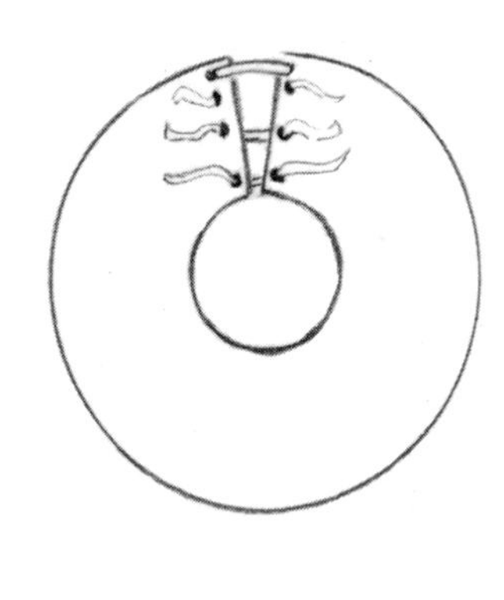

Diagram of collar when not in use

PRUDENCE WALKER

This diagram shows an Elizabethan collar in place, and details of its construction. It is used to prevent a dog from chewing or biting himself.

dogs frequently revert to an almost wild state at such times and it becomes hazardous to approach, let alone touch, them when they are injured.

An attempt must be made to approach the injured animal but it should be made with caution, and without nervousness. Speak to the dog all the time in a soft, reassuring tone, and watch his eyes and head reflexes to assess how he is responding. If he is in pain, yet conscious, he will probably snarl and attempt to warn you off. It is best to apply a muzzle, and a good one can be improvised with a strip of cloth, say about two inches wide and 36 inches long. Use a necktie in an emergency. Form a loop in the center and slip it over his nose down to his lower jaws and draw it tight. Take the loose ends to the back of his head and tie them in a bow-knot behind the ears. He will then be unable to bite. If he is not already there, get him onto his right side by holding him at the scruff of his neck and easing his hind legs from under him. Should he, owing to the pain, continue to struggle, it may be necessary to immobilize him further by tying his front legs together, then his hind legs. This will render him less hysterical and keep him from complicating his injuries.

A very small dog can sometimes be quieted by throwing a blanket or coat over his head and gathering him up in that. Large dogs are often a problem because of their size and ferocity when in intense pain. In that case it may be necessary to lasso the head from the vantage point afforded by a doorway, or a fence or gate if outdoors. The dog can then be pulled close up against the door to be dealt with. If a helper is available, and the dog is large and vicious, the assistent should utilize a second lasso. This permits pull to be exerted from opposite directions, and the dog will be held immobile. One rope should then be tied to a solid object, while the other can be tightened to restrain the patient while a muzzle is applied, and the feet tied.

Broken Bones

Two kinds of breaks are usual – one being a simple fracture, where the bone is broken but remains in position, the other a compound fracture where the bone ends are displaced so that they do not touch, and the end or ends protrude through the skin. This is the more serious condition, requiring a veterinarian at once, not only to relieve the animal's pain but to set the leg properly. Even if only bruised, a dog will limp and evince considerable pain. So, if you are in doubt as to whether a bone is broken, run your fingers gently down his leg for any bump or apparent dislocation. A check on the opposite leg will give you a comparision to go by. An X-Ray may be necessary in some cases, and your veterinarian will have the equipment for making this. A "green-stick" fracture as a rule occurs with young puppies. The break is not transverse, but longitudinal.

If you decide to apply first aid, assuming that qualified help will not arrive for some time, the simplest form of splint consists of two rigid slats or sticks which are light in weight and cut to a suitable length. These are laid on either side of the damaged leg and lashed securely above and below the suspected point of break. This will hold the leg firmly and if the dog continues to thrash about in panic, the splint will keep the sharp ends of the bones from piercing the skin or a vital blood vessel. If you have absorbent cotton available before you apply the splints, put this around the leg first, then wrap around it entirely with a wide bandage.

If the dog's tail has been broken, and this happens sometimes to dogs caught in a closing car door, follow the same method. Splint

PURINA PET CARE CENTER

Accidents, particularly with puppies, can take the most unusual shapes and forms. Therefore, it is well to be prepared. Fortunately, this puppy was rescued in time.

immediately, for a healed kinked tail is unsightly, particularly in the Beagle.

Cuts and Wounds

The best cure is the dog's tongue itself. Not only does it clean out the foreign matter in the wound, but the saliva is slightly antiseptic. However, the wound may be too serious for this, or the spot may be inaccessible. If so, you will need to deal with the matter yourself. If the dog is in pain and uncooperative muzzle him before proceeding. Swab the whole area of the wound with clean warm water to which a mild antiseptic like peroxide has been added. If stitches are needed, your veterinarian will have to be called in. Should bleeding be excessive and unresponsive to the usual coagulants like granulated sugar, powdered alum, or a styptic pencil it may be necessary to apply a tourniquet or pressure bandage.

Pressure Bandage

The conventional bandage is intended to protect an area from contamination by foreign matter, to prevent rubbing off and loss of applied medications and to absorb any oozing of pus.

A pressure bandage is applied primarily to stop bleeding. In order to perform this function it must be wound tightly. This will usually impede circulation. Therefore, a pressure bandage should not be left unattended for more than a few hours and it should be removed immediately if the area above the bandage becomes puffy and swollen. In every case it should be loosened within twelve hours.

Usually a pad of absorbent cotton is applied to the wound. Then the bandage is wound tightly about the area. The task is completed by covering the bandage with a layer of adhesive tape.

Tourniquet

Bleeding quite often frightens the layman far out of proportion to the dog's actual loss of blood. Nevertheless, excessive bleeding is dangerous and it may be wise to apply a tourniquet. A strong cord or strip of cloth can be used, but a necktie or shoelace is often more handy. Ascertain whether the blood is issuing from a vein or artery. Arterial blood is bright crimson and pulsates out of the body, venous blood is darker and flows steadily. If the wound involves an artery, the tourniquet should be applied between the artery and the heart; whereas, if the blood flows from a vein, the tourniquet should be applied to the far side of the wound from the heart. Take the tourniquet cloth and tie it around the leg, rather loosely, with a secure knot. Then insert a small stick or rod through the loop and twist or turn it until the flow of blood has stopped. The pressure should only be maintained for five to ten minutes at a time, then loosened and re-applied at once. This will prevent any damaging effect from the loss of circulation.

Shock

A dog will frequently suffer from shock after an accident or a severe blow on the head. The natural "anaesthetic" which comes with shock is an advantage, although accompanied by low pulse and shallow respiration. The dog will be cold to the touch and may exhibit excessive thirst along with panting and extreme trepidation. Or, on the contrary, the pulse may be too rapid. Whatever the symptoms they will be rather disturbing and make the onlookers anxious to give the dog immediate aid. The first thing is to cover the dog with a blanket or coat and let him generate some body heat beneath it. Keep him quiet, preferably in a darkened room, resting on his right side. He is likely to be conscious, although very weak. Do not give any stimulants if an internal injury is suspected, but if this seems unlikely, the patient can have a little Karo Syrup dissolved in warm milk every five or ten minutes, provided his is conscious and no vomiting takes place.

Electric Shock

Loose electric wires and open wall sockets offer great temptation to young puppies, especially those who reconnoiter a room for the first time. A loose lamp cord is likely to be chewed and once the insulation has been pierced by the sharp puppy teeth, the youngster will almost certainly be badly burned about the mouth if the wire is live. Worse, he may urinate with fright and be electrocuted if he is close to some metal conductor onto which his water seeps.

The first thing to do is switch off the electricity, making sure that you make no contact with the water or the live wire. If it is impossible to switch off the current, use a wooden stick or similar non-conductor to remove the wire from the puppy's mouth or to edge him away from the area. Artificial respiration should be given if he is inert and even if he seems dead. Place the animal on his side and press down on his ribs, releasing suddenly. Repeat this every 20 seconds, stopping occasionally to see if breathing has re-started. Once it has, cease the resuscitation, and follow up with the treatment given for shock.

Transporting an Injured Dog

Place an open blanket or wide board alongside the patient, and then ease and edge it under his recumbent body, preferably with the help of an assistant. The blanket or board can then be utilized as a stretcher to carry the dog to more convenient place where veterinary assistance can be secured.

Poisoning

Always try and pin point the poison your dog has ingested. If you know the poison and can find the container in which it came, the antidote will be printed on the label. If you do not know the poison, describe the symptoms carefully over the telephone to your veterinarian; he may recognize it and advise on first-aid measures.

Here is a list of the poisons likely to be encountered:

Arsenic: This is usually an ingredient in rat and vermin poisons. The symptoms are abdominal pain, loss of appetite, vomiting, diarrhea, great depression, accelerated breathing, and eventual collapse. An effective antidote is Epsom salts (one teaspoonful in water) followed by lime or barley water, egg whites beaten in milk, diluted olive oil. A solution of iron sulphate with magnesium oxide is very effective; any druggist can prepare this for you to keep on hand in your first-aid kit.

Acids: These cause excessive salivation and rapid deterioration. The type of vomit and breath odor will sometimes give the clue to the kind of acid. Bicarbonate of soda is effective, so is chalk and water, or plenty of milk of magnesia. Hydrocyanic acid is found in the laurel leaf, also in the wild cherry. Since these are often encountered in gardens or on walks, they constitute a menace to the puppy with an under-developed sense of taste. The poison acts quickly, but if caught immediately, two tablespoonful of corn syrup or dextrose may save the dog.

Alkalies: These are commonly found in such household cleansing agents as lye and kitchen cleansers. Vinegar or lemon juice are good antidotes for they neutralize the caustic content. The symptoms are excessive salivation, followed by nausea and intense pain.

Lead: This is usually taken in the from of paint, licking or drinking from old paint tins, occasionally from horticultural lead arsenate sprays. The main symptom is a bluish discoloration of the gum margin. The best antidotes are Epsom salts (one soupspoonful in half a cup of warm water), dilute sulphuric acid, or potassium iodide. High saline irrigation is important.

Mercury: This is absorbed as a rule from licking at skin ointments composed of bichloride of mercury or coal-tar derivatives, from mange lotion or rat poisons. Antidotes are whites of eggs beaten up in milk or water (before and after the emetic), dilute sulphuric acid, gluten of wheat or potassium iodide.

Phosphorus: Found in rat poisons, or when puppies have played with and eaten unstruck matches. A slow acting poison, the symptoms are stomach pains, restlessness, swelling of the tongue, jaundice and weakness. The vomit is of a greenish brown color and glows in the dark. Do *not* give oily or fatty substances; even cream or milk should be avoided as these increase the solubility of the poison. Give peroxide, diluted half in half with water – about one ounce for each ten pounds of dog.

Strychnine: This is the poison commonly used by dog poisoners and its effect is cruel. Symptoms are muscle twitch, convulsions and body paralysis, with eyes protruding. The poison is used in some rat poisons. Fast action is necessary if the dog is to be saved; a powerful emetic such as an injection of apomorphine by your veterinarian to cause vomiting followed by pentabarbital, although chloral hydrate and amyl nitrate are effective too. All must be administered by a veterinarian. First aid entails an immediate emetic like peroxide, and keeping the patient in a dark room. Butter, pork drippings or similar fats are useful.

There are many other poisons which the dog can come by, some of specific nature like the foregoing, others more general like food poisoning, which a dog can pick up from a refuse or a garbage can. Even the best fed and cared for dogs are fascinated by such spots. Whatever the poison, the first thing is to induce vomiting. The following list of household emetics, immediate antidotes for poison, should be posted:

1. Common washing soda: A lump about the size of a hazelnut should be administered like a pill.
2. Common salt: Mix two teaspoonsful in a cup of warm water.
3. Mustard: One tablespoonful in a cup of warm water.
4. Hydrogen peroxide: This is very effective. Mix equal parts of hydrogen peroxide and water and administer one and one-half tablespoonsful for each pounds of weight. Vomiting quickly follows.

Most of the advice given here, will, we hope, be superfluous. Many Beagles go all through life without encountering any of these problems. However this chapter, and the preceding one (Disease) were written in the belief that knowledge is reassuring in itself. It gives one the self-confidence that he will be capable of handling an emergency situation should one arise.

Fish Hooks

Don't try to pull the hook back out. Cut it off as close as possible and push it through. Use antiseptic.

Porcupine Quills

Beagles sometimes encounter porcupines and end up stuck with quills. It usually happens in a place far from veterinary help. So if you are going into woods known to be porcupine country better take along a pair of electrician's pliers. First chain the dog and hold him standing while you pull the quills from one side – pull! no matter how painful. He can then be laid on that side. Work on his mouth next, and his tongue. Then around his eyes. Next behind the shoulders and the belly to prevent quills from working into vital organs. Consider this merely first aid. Get the dog to the vet's as fast as possible. Quills that work themselves in will have to be removed under anesthetic.

"In Conclusion".

HOUNDS & HUNTING

In Conclusion

In writing this book, I have endeavored to show you the advantages of the Beagle as a dog for the family circle. Without doubt he will make you an ideal pet; if he turns out a fine specimen and you aspire to the joys and interests of the show ring you will look forward to many hours of pleasurable entertainment. The main thing is that you will own a *proper* dog – one whose honest background and history, completely unadulterated by the uninformed "improvers" that some other breeds possess, will endear him to you. Whether your interest extends to the fields and streams or remains indoors, your Beagle will conform to please you. Few breeds can offer their owners a slice of both worlds. Your Beagle can do this and more for he is an excellent all purpose dog.

Appendix

Dog Talk

Through the years dog aficionados have developed their own jargòn. Some of these terms, such as "blocky" have passed into everyday speech; others, such as "apron" or "balance", are commonly used words adapted to dog purposes.

Use of such words in doggy conversation is almost mandatory for the dog lover. Understanding of their meaning will contribute to his enjoyment of dog books and articles. The author has endeavored to minimize the use of dog world jargon in this book. However, some of the terms are so beautifully descriptive that they could not be omitted.

While not all of the terms defined in this glossary apply to Beagles, they are included because a dog lover does not restrict his affection and understanding to one breed; his love embraces them all.

Affixes: These are normally, attached to a dog's registered name so that he can be identified with a particular kennel. Properly, an affix should be divided into prefix (when the kennel name goes before the dog's name) and suffix (when the kennel name goes after the dog's name).

Almond eyes: Eyes set in tissue of almond shape.

Angulations: Angles formed where the bones meet: shoulder, upper arm, hock, stifle.

Apple-head: A head which is rounded on top of the skull as in the Toy Spaniels. An undesirable feature in most breeds.

Apron: The frill or long hair below the neck on long-coated dogs.

B or b: Abbreviation for bitch (female) as described in show catalogs, race cards, etc.

Bad doer: A dog who does badly however well fed and cared for. Often one who has never done well from birth.

Bad show-er A dog who will not or cannot display himself well at shows. May be due to contrariness, nerves or boredom.

Balance: Coordination of the muscles giving graceful action coupled with the overall conformation of the dog. The lateral dimensions of the dog should mold pleasingly with the horizontal and vertical dimensions.

Barrel: Refers to the rib cage. This should be strong and well-rounded, permitting plenty of heart room. The opposite to ribs that are flat-sided, lacking spring.

Bat ears: Large erect ears like those of a bat, as in the French Bulldog. A fault in many other breeds.

Bay: The voice of a hound on the trail.

B. B.: Best of Breed abbreviation.

Beard: The profuse, rather bushy whiskers of the Brussels Griffon, not the terrier.

Beefy: Heavy development of the hindquarters.

Belton: The blue and white and orange and white-flecked color seen in certain English Setters. This is called ticking in Beagles.

Bench show: Dog show where the dogs competing are "benched" or leashed on benches.

Bitchy: Refers to an effeminate or ultra-refined male dog.

Bite: Relative position of the lower and upper teeth when mouth is shut.

Blaze: A white (usually bulbous) marking running up the center of the face of some dogs.

Bloom: Glossiness or good sheen of coat, especially desirable in a smooth-coated breed.

Blocky: Term used to describe a head which is cube-shaped, as in the Boston Terrier.

Blue: A blue-gray, such color as might be seen in the Whippet or Bedlington.

Bobtail: A naturally tailless dog. Often used for the Old English Sheepdog.

Bone: A well-boned dog is one having limbs giving an appearance and feel of strength and spring without coarseness.

Br.: Breeder, that is the owner of the dog's dam at the time of whelping.

B. R. or br.: Blue Roan, a mixture of blue and white in which the colors are blended about equally.

Brace: Two dogs or two dogs exhibited together.

Breeching: The tan hairs on the backs and thighs of such a breed as the Manchester Terrier.

Brindle: A mixture of dark and light hairs giving a generally dark effect, usually being lighter streaks on a gray, tawny, brown or black background. Found in Scottish Terriers and the Bull Breeds especially.

Brisket: That part of the body in front of the chest and between the forelegs.

Broken Color: Where the main coat color is broken up by white or other hairs.

Broken-haired: Roughed-up wiry coat.

Broken-up face: Any face which shows a combination of lay-back, projecting lower jaw and wrinkle. Seen in the Pekingese, Bulldog and Pug.

Brood Bitch: A female kept for breeding purposes. Brood matron.

B. S.: Best in Show or Best in Sex. A dog who has beaten all others or all others in his sex, respectively.

Brush: A tail which has long bushy hair such as seen in the Spitz breeds.

Burr: The irregular formation inside the ear.

Butterfly Nose: The nostrils are mottled or show flesh color among the black or brown pigment.

Button Ears: Ears which drop over in front covering the inner cavity, such as in the Fox Terrier.

Bye: After dogs have been paired at field trials, the odd dog remaining.

Cat Foot: A compact and round foot, well held together, like the foot of a cat.

C. C.: Challenge Certificate. A Kennel Club award signed by the judge for the best dog of his sex in breed at a Championship Show.

C. D.: Companion Dog. One holding this degree has passed a test for obedience and character reliability.

C. D. X.: Companion Dog (Excellent). A degree indicating that the holder has passed a test for obedience and character reliability.

Champion: A dog that has been awarded his Championship by the AKC, after defeating a number of dogs in competitive judgings.

Character: A combination of the essential points of appearance and disposition contributing to the whole, and distinctive to the particular variety of dog to which the holder belongs.

Cheeky: Full, thick cheeks.

China Eye: A blue, wall eye.

Choke collar: A leather or chain collar that tightens or loosens according to the hand controlling it.

Chops: These pendulous and upper lips common to the Bulldog and some hounds.

Gloddy: A low and very thick-set build.

Chun Red: A rich coppery shade popular in the Pekingese, named after the famous Champion "Goodwood Chun".

Close Coupled: Short or closely knit between the last ribs and the hip joints.

Close Lying: A coat, in which the body hair lies flat and snug on the body.

C. M.: Certificate of Merit. An award to Field Trial competitors of outstanding merit but not prize winners.

Cobby: Of compact, neat and muscular formation (like a cob horse).

Companion Dog: (C.D.): Also, Companion Dog Excellent (C.D.X.); Utility Dog (U.D.); Tracking Dog (T.D.); Titles awarded in Obedience Trials.

Condition: General health, coat and appearance.

Confirmation: The form and structure and arrangement of parts in conformance with the Breed Standard.

Corky: Compact, nimble in body and mind, lively and spirited.

Coupling: That part of the body between the last ribs and the hip joints, joined by the backbone.

Couple: Two hounds.

Cow-hocked: A dog is said to be cow-hocked when his hocks are bent inwards, thus throwing the hind feet outwards. A fault in any breed, even in the Pyrenean Mountain Dog and present-day St. Bernard.

Crank-tail: A screw tail.

Chest: The upper arched part of a dog's neck.

Cropping: The practice of cutting or trimming a dog's ears to make them small and/or stand erect in various defined shapes. The practice is common in Europe, but illegal in Britain and some American states.

Crossbred: A dog whose parents are of different breeds.

Croup: The area adjacent to the sacrum and immediately before the root of the tail.

Cryptorchid: The adult dog whose testicles are abnormally retained in the abdominal cavity.

Culotte: The feathery tail on the back of the forelegs of the Pekingese, Pomeranian and Schipperke.

Cushion: The fullness of the foreface given by the padding of the upper lips in the Mastiff and Bulldog.

D or d: The abbreviation for the male dog as described in show catalogs, race cards, etc.

Dam: The female parent of puppies. The term is generally used but has special reference to a bitch from the time of her whelping a litter to the weaning of her last puppy in that litter.

Dappled: A term usual in Dachshunds. It means a variegated or mottled color; usually small, confluent blotches of silver with tan, black or black-and-tan.

Derby: Field trial competition for young dogs.

Dewclaws: The rudimentary fifth digit and claws found on the insides of the legs below the hocks, which are better removed a few days after birth.

Dewlap: The loose pendulous skin under the throat as in the Bloodhound.

Dish-faced: When a depression in the nasal bone makes the nose higher in the tip than at the stop.

Dimples: The shallow depressions at each side of the breastbone, as in the Dachshund.

Docking: Shortening the dog's tail by amputation.

Dome: The term which refers to the rounded skull of some dogs, as the Spaniel.

Double coat: The outer coat is weather-resistant and protective. Inner coat is of softer hair for warmth.

Down-faced: When the tip of the nose curves well below the level of the stop. Opposite to dish-faced.

Down In Pastern: Showing an angle of the front feet forward and outward instead of straight in line from the forearm to the ground in those breeds which require this formation.

Drop Ears: Ears which are pendant and hanging close and flat to the side of the cheek.

Dual Champion: In England this is one who has not only reached Championship status in the show ring but has qualified for a working certificate as a gun-dog in the field. In America such a dog would be known as a "bench and field Champion".

Dudley Nose: Wholly flesh-color nostrils, usually cherry or coffee-colored; quite distinct from Butterfly Nose.

Elbow: The joint at the top of the forearm.

Elbow-out: Elbows not close to the body, as those of the Bulldog. A fault in most other breeds.

Expression: A combination of the position, size, color and luster of the eyes, giving the countenance the desired distinction peculiar to the particular variety of dog.

Fall: The long hair overhanging the face in the Skye and Yorkshire Terriers.

False Heat: Not uncommon in bitches. The animal will give every sign of expecting, even experiencing a heat, but these will not persist for the length of time of a normal period and she will revert or "go off" very quickly. When a bitch with a false heat is mated it usually proves unfruitful.

Fancier: One who is actively interested in some phase of dogdom.

Feather, Featherings: The long hair fringing on the back of the legs of some breeds such as Spaniels and Setters. The term is loosely applied to include ear fringes and tail flag.

Felted: When a coat becomes matted.

Fetch: To retrieve.

Fiddle Head:	A long wolfish head.
Field Trial:	Competition in which dogs are judged on ability in following a trail or retrieving game.
Filled-up Face:	One in which the cheek muscles are well developed, such as in the Staffordshire.
Flag:	The long, fine, silky hairs under the tails of Setters and some Retrievers, graduating in length from long at the root to short at the tip of the tail.
Flank:	Side between the last rib and hip.
Flecked:	When the coat is lightly ticked with another color, yet not roaned, spotted or dappled.
Flews:	The pendulous inner corners of the lips of the upper jaw.
Frill:	The hair under the neck and on the chest.
Fringes:	See Feathering.
Fly-ears:	Semi-erect ears which stand out from the side of the head.
Front:	Strictly speaking all that can be seen from the front except the head, but having special reference to the brisket and forelegs.
Forelock:	The abundant tassle of hair grown on the forehead, which falls over towards the eyes rather like a cap, such as in the Kerry Blue Terrier.
Frog-face:	A face in which the nose is extended and the jaw recedes, with special reference to short-face breeds.
Furrow:	The groove or indentation running in a median line from the stop to near the occiput.
Gait:	How a dog walks, trots or runs.
Gay Tail:	One which from root to tip is carried above the horizontal.

Good Doer:	A dog who does well without any special treatment, and who has thrived from birth.
Good Show-er:	A dog who displays himself to perfection at the show regardless of his general condition.
Goose-Rump:	A sloping croup which falls away too abruptly, the tail being on too low.
Grizzle:	An iron-gray coat color.
Groups:	The six divisions into which the AKC has grouped all breeds: Sporting Dogs; Hounds; Working Dogs; Terriers; Toys; Non-Sporting Dogs.
Guide Dog:	A dog trained to guide blind people. Usually a bitch of the German Shepherd, Retriever, Airedale or Collie breeds.
Gun-shy:	A dog which is fearful at the sight of a gun or its report.
Gun-dog:	Dog trained to find live game and retrieve it when shot.
Handler:	A person who handles dogs at shows. It applies to any one who does this, but it usually refers to a professional or highly trained handler.
Hard-mouthed:	A dog is said to be hard-mouthed when he damages the game he retrieves. The term is in special reference to Gun-dogs.
Hare Feet:	Feet which are rather long and narrow with the toes well separated as in the Hare.
Harlequin:	Pied or patched black and white coat, referring specially to a type of Great Dane.
Haw:	An inner eye-lid more developed in some breeds than in others. It hangs open and shows red in such breeds as the Great Dane and Bloodhound.

H. C.:	Highly Commended. An award granted to an exhibit of outstanding merit but which generally carries with it no monetary award and stands sixth in placing.
Heat:	A bitch is said to be "in heat" during her oestral period, when she is in season, or menstruating.
Height:	The height of a dog is usually measured perpendicularly from the ground to the withers, i.e. to the top of the shoulders.
H. M.:	Hound Marked. When the body patches conform to the conventional pattern of hounds, i.e., a dark saddle (usually black), dark ears and head (usually tan), and often a patch about the set-on or on the upper limbs, the rest of the dog being white.
Hocks:	The joints in the hind legs between the pasterns and stifles, similar to the ankle in humans.
Huckle Bones:	The top of the hip joints.
In-Breeding:	The mating of closely related dogs. This is done to perpetuate certain characteristics which are considered desirable and which already exist to some extent. (See relevant paragraph).
Int. Ch.:	International Champion. A dog who has been awarded the title of champion in more than one country. It is not an officially recognized term by The Kennel Club.
Keel:	The absolute base of a Dachshund body with special reference to the brisket.
Kink-Tail:	A tail with a break or a kink in it.
Layback:	The receding nose found in some of the short-faced breeds.
Leash:	A thong by which dogs are held. An

	obsolete term for three Greyhounds.
Leather:	The skin of the ear-flap. It is sometimes trimmed to make neat or to prevent a hound from getting his ears torn in the chase.
Leggy:	So high on the leg that the dog appears assymetrical.
Level Jaws:	When the jaws are so placed that the teeth meet about evenly, neither undershot nor noticeably overshot.
Line-breeding:	The mating of dogs of similar strains not too closely related. (See relevant paragraph).
Lippy.	When the lips overhang or are developed more than they should.
Litter:	Collective term for the puppies born to the bitch at the same whelping.
Liver:	A color – deep reddish brown.
Loaded shoulders	Heaviness in shoulders.
Loins:	That part of the body protecting the lower viscera, between the last ribs and hindquarters.
Long Coupled:	The reverse to close coupled. Dachshunds would be termed long-coupled dogs.
Lumber:	Too much flesh, ungainly in appearance and clumsy in action. Does not apply to puppies.
Lurcher:	A crossbred hound.
Maiden:	In the general sense an un-mated bitch, but in exhibition world language a dog or bitch not having won a first-prize.
Mane:	An abundance of long hair around the top of the neck.
Mask:	The dark markings on the muzzle in some breeds, or the muzzle itself.
Match show:	A form of competition which is arranged more or less privately by members of local and breed societies

	to discuss and compare special points in the specimens presented.
Mating:	An act by which a bitch is served in copulation by a stud dog. A service.
Matron:	A brood bitch. One kept for breeding purposes.
Merle:	Bluish-grey color marbled with black, seen in working Sheepdogs.
Miscellaneous Class	The class at dog shows for dogs of certain specified breeds for which no regular classification exists.
Molera:	Incomplete ossification of the skull. Characteristic of Chihuahuas.
Monorchid:	A dog with one descended testicle. See Cryptorchid.
Muzzle:	Foreface of the dog: nasal bone, nostrils, jaws, Also a strap or wire cage attached to the dog.
N. F. C.:	Not For Competition. Used when a dog is entered at a show purely for display not for competition.
Novice:	Generally an amateur or professional breeder of little experience. A beginner or tyro. Also a class distinction classification for a dog or bitch not having won two first prizes.
Occiput:	The part of the skull at the top of the back of the head which is prominent in most of the Hound group.
Oestrum:	The menstrual period. A bitch experiencing oestral flow is said to be "in heat" or "in season", that is, she is sexually excited and ripe for service by a male dog.
On His Toes:	The term indicates that a dog is alert and exhibiting himself well.
Otter Tail:	A tail which is thick at the roots and tapers away like that of an otter. Seen in some Retrievers.
Out At Elbows:	Having the joints of the elbow turned

out and away from the side of the body, due to faulty front formation.

Outcross: The mating of unrelated dogs or those of an entirely different strain (see relevant paragraph).

Out At Shoulders: Having the shoulders protruding outwards so as to increase the width of the front, as in the Bulldog.

Overshot: Having the upper incisors projecting over and beyond the lower incisors.

Pace: A gait which promotes a rolling motion of the body.

Pack: Several hounds kept together. Mixed pack is made up of males and females.

Pad: The cushioned sole of the foot.

Parti-color: A coat of two or more colors in patches.

Pastern: The lowest part of the leg, below the knee on the foreleg or below the hock on the hind leg.

Peak: The term applied to the occiput when it is prominent, but rightly restricted to use with Basset Hounds, Bloodhounds and some Setters.

Pedigree: A table of genealogy, giving the names of the dog's ancestors.

Pencilling: The thin, dark elegant lines on the surface of the toes of some breeds, as in the English Toy Terrier.

Pied: A term used for a dog having two coat colors in *unequal* proportions: mainly white with large black patches or brindle sections placed irregularly over the body. Sometimes referred to as Piebald. When the patches are golden or red brindle, the term used is Skewbald.

Pig-jaw: Badly overshot jaw.

Pile: The thick undercoat of a medium or

long-coated dog.

Piley: A coat that contains both soft and hard hair, as in the Dandie Dinmont Terrier.

Plume: The soft hair on the tails of both the Pekingese and Pomeranian, this being long and feathery.

Pompon: A rounded tuft of hair on the tail (Poodle). Sometimes miscalled Pom-Pom.

Prefix: A particular kennel's name which is entered before a dog's name to identify it with that kennel.

Premium list: An announcement sent to prospective exhibitors in a forthcoming dog show, containing list of awards.

Prick Ears: Ears which stand erect.

Puppy: A dog under 12 months of age.

Quarterings: The junctions of the limbs, especially the hindquarters.

Racy: Slight in build and rather long-bodied.

Rangy: Rather elongated in body and loose-limbed. Having rather more substance than one who is racy.

Red: A general term for several colors, ranging from fallow or fawn down to copper.

Reserve: Usually the fourth place after judging.

Ribbed Up: A compact dog with the ribs nicely barrelled and placed.

Ring: The area in which exhibits are handled and placed before a judge at the show. In most cases it is rectangular in spite of its name.

Ring Tail: A curled tail which describes an almost complete circle.

Roach Back: One that arches upwards from the withers along the spine with particular emphasis about the loins.

Roan: A mixture of white with another color (usually blue or red) in about equal proportions and showing good blending.

Rose Ears: Ears which fold over, exposing the inner burr.

R. R. or r.r.: Red Roan. A mixture of red and white in which the colors are blended about equally.

Ruff: The frill or apron of long stand-off hair, usually coarse, around the neck of some breeds, such as the Chow Chow.

Sable: When the outer coat is shaded with black over a light undercoat, a dog is said to be of sable color, as in Collies.

Saddle: A rectangular marking of black on the back extending to the upper flanks.

Sanction Show: A show held under special rules for Members of a club and sanctioned by a Kennel Club.

Scent: Odor left by an animal on the trail (ground scent) or wafted in the air (airborne scent).

Screw Tail: A tail which is short and rapidly tapered to a point, and is twisted or screwed, as in some Bulldogs and Boston Terriers.

Season: When a bitch menstruates she is said to be "in season".

Second Mouth: A dog has his second mouth when the first or milk teeth are replaced by the second or permanent teeth.

Second Thighs: The muscular development of the legs between the stifles and the hocks.

Self color: One color or whole color except for

shading.

Self-marked: When a dog is all one color.

Semi-prick ears: Ears carried erect with tips bending forward.

Septum: The very thin dividing bone between the nostrils.

Service: The term given to the act of copulation when a bitch is served by a stud dog. A "free service" is one given by courtesy of the owner of a stud dog following an unsuccessful service for which a fee has been paid.

Set-on: Where the root of the tail is set on to the body.

Shelly: Having a narrow and shallow body, but not necessarily lacking in bone and substance.

Shoulders: The point at which the height of a dog is measured, about the top of the shoulder blades.

Sickle hocks: Hocks which are both well let down and well bent, as in most racily built breeds.

Sickle tail: One which describes a semi-circle and is usually gay.

Sire: The male parent of a litter of puppies.

Sloping shoulders Those which are well laid back and therefore angulated to a more or less marked degree.

Smooth coat: Short hair, close-lying.

Snipy: When the dog's muzzle is weak and too long and narrow.

Soft mouth: A dog with a soft mouth is one who can retrieve game without damaging it. It is especially applied to Gundogs.

Soundness: The state of the dog's physical and mental health when everything is functioning normally.

Splay feet: Those feet in which the toes are spread wide apart, as in some feet employed to work on marshy ground.

Spay: A surgical operation to prevent conception.

Spread: The distance covered by the wide-apart forelegs of a Bulldog. The exaggerated front of any out-at-shoulders dog.

Spring: Elasticity. Spring of rib is when the ribs are well rounded, sound and elastic; spring of back means its ability to return to its normal after pressure is removed from that area.

Squirrel tail: One which curves forward over the back even from the root, as in some short-tailed terriers.

Stance: Way of standing.

Standard: The official description of the ideal dog, by which dogs are judged at shows.

Stand off: The ruff or frill of rather coarse hair which stands off or away from the neck of the Spitz breeds.

Staring coat: When the hair is dry, harsh, curling at the tips.

Stern: The tail. A term used mainly in Beagle, Harrier, and Foxhound circles.

Stifle: The joint in the hind leg joining the first and second thighs and corresponding to the human knee.

Stop: The depression or stop between and in front of the eyes, approximating to the bridge of the nose in humans.

String: A tail which is quite thin, even at the root, and tapers away to a fine point, as in the Irish Water Spaniel.

Stud book: A record of the breeding particulars of recognized breeds.

Straight hocks:	Those which are practically vertical, lacking bend.
Straight shoulders:	Those which are not laid back and lack angulation.
Stud dog:	A male dog kept partly or solely for breeding purposes and for whose services the owner charges a stud fee.
Sway back:	One which through spinal defects or poor muscular development sags in the middle.
Team:	Three or more dogs of one breed.
T.:	Ticked.
T. A. F.:	Transfer applied for.
T. D.:	Tracking dog. One who has passed a test in tracking.
Throaty:	A dog is said to be throaty when he carries an excess of loose skin about the throat.
Thumb marks:	The round black spots on the forelegs about the pasterns on the Manchester Terrier and English Toy Terrier.
Ticked:	When small elongated specks of another color appear on the main body color.
Tie:	The term used in reference to the locking of dog and bitch during the mating union.
Tiger brindle:	A mixture of dark and light hairs among which the dark color forms a series of stripes or has the resemblance of stripes.
Timber:	Another name for bone. Good bone formation especially in the legs.
Tongue:	To give tongue is to give voice or bark.
Top-knot:	The long fluffy hair on the top of the head of some breeds.
Trace:	The dark line which runs down the spine of some shortcoated breeds.

Tricolor: A dog of three different colors, generally black, white and tan.

Trousers: The hair on the hindquarters of some breeds, notably the Afghan.

Tucked-up: When the loins are well lifted-up, as in the Greyhound.

Tulip ears: Those ears which are carried erect, and lean slightly forwards.

Turn-up: The projecting turned-up chin of the Bulldog.

Type: That quality essential to a dog if he is to represent or approximate the ideal model of his breed based upon the Standard of the breed.

U.D.: Utility dog. A dog trained for general services work.

Undercoat: The soft, furry wool beneath the outer coat present in many breeds and sometimes of a different color.

Undershot: Having the lower incisors projecting beyond the upper incisors, due to a malformation of the jaw, as in the Bulldog.

Unsound: An unsound dog is one who is unhealthy or below average in general condition, working ability, movement or character. The unsoundness may be temporary or permanent, partial or complete. A bitch, after whelping, is temporarily unsound by being out of coat, etc. A deformed or unreliable dog is more or less permanently unsound.

Varminty: A very bright or piercing expression.

Vent: The tan colored hair situated under the tail of some breeds such as the Manchester Terrier. In a broader sense it is the area immediately surrounding the anus.

V. H. C.: Very highly commended. An award

granted to an exhibit of outstanding merit, but which generally carries no monetary prize with it. The award is fifth in order of placing.

Wall eyes: Those which are parti-colored white-and-blue, normally seen in merle Sheepdogs and Collies and Cardiganshire Welsh Corgis.

Weedy: Very lightly formed and lacking in substance.

Well sprung: Well formed, with particular emphasis on chest development and spring of rib. When ribs are well rounded, sound and elastic, a dog is said to be well sprung.

Wheaten: Color fawn or pale yellow.

Wheel back: Another term for the arched or convex back.

Whelping: The act of giving birth to puppies.

Whelps: Newly born puppies.

Whip tail: A tail which is stiff and straight, as in the Pointer when in action.

Whipcord tail: One which is much too thin for the breed of dog to which it is attached. Distinct from the "string" tail of the Irish Water Spaniel.

Whole color: One which covers the whole body as in red or black Cocker Spaniels.

Withers: That point where the neck joins the body, about the shoulders.

Working certificate: A certificate awarded to Gun-dogs at Field Trials where they have proved that they are trained and capable of carrying out the work for which they are bred. This award is necessary for any Gun-dog who is already a Show Champion and is required to be a Dual Champion.

Wrinkle: Loosely folded skin on the forehead and cheeks.